PRODUCTION MANAGEMENT
MAKING SHOWS HAPPEN

A PRACTICAL GUIDE

PRODUCTION MANAGEMENT
Making Shows Happen

Peter Dean

The Crowood Press

First published in 2002 by
The Crowood Press Ltd
Ramsbury, Marlborough
Wiltshire SN8 2HR

British Library Cataloguing-in-Publication Data
A catalogue record for this book is available from the
British Library.

ISBN 1 86126 451 8

Disclaimer

Safety is of the utmost importance in every aspect of theatre
work. When using tools and other equipment, you should
always follow the manufacturer's recommended procedures
closely. The author and publisher cannot accept responsibility
for any accident or injury caused by following any of the advice
given in this book.

Line artwork by Annette Findlay

Designed and edited by Focus Publishing,
11a St Botolph's Road,
Sevenoaks
Kent TN13 3AJ

Printed and bound in Great Britain by
Antony Rowe Ltd, Chippenham, Wiltshire.

Acknowledgements

I would like to thank the Guildhall School of Music &
Drama for the independent research grant that made my
work on this book possible. Also all the creative teams,
technicians and stage management I have worked with
over the years for their enthusiasm, support, skills and
ideas, many of which are described in this book. David
Edwards and everyone at Derby Playhouse during my time
there. All technical theatre staff and students on the
BA(Hons) in Stage Management and Technical Theatre at
Guildhall for allowing me to photograph their work.
Christina Whellams for her help with proof reading and
her IT skills with charts and spreadsheets. The theatres I
have worked in for allowing me to learn from my mistakes,
while using their budgets and resources. And finally my
wife, Arabella, for her support, constant help and advice.

Special thanks to the designers and lighting designers
whose work is featured in this book.

Photographic Acknowledgements

All photographs are by the author except where indicated
otherwise.
Front cover: Our Country's Good, GSMD drama
production. Designer: Sue Mayes; lighting designer: Rob
Halliday; directed by Stephen Jameson.
Back cover: The Snowmaiden, GSMD opera production.
Set designer: Isabella Bywater; lighting designer: Simon
Corder; costume designer: Sophie Bugeaud; directed by:
Stephen Medcalf.

CONTENTS

1   What is Production Management? 6

2   Who Does What in the Theatre? 10

3   The Production Manager's Team 29

4   The Pre-Production Process 67

5   Working Safely 88

6   Rehearsing the Show 110

7   Preparing the Show 125

8   The Production Week 143

Appendix I: Codes of Practice for Theatre Access Equipment ..177

Appendix II: Health and Safety Legislation 184

Glossary 188

Index 191

1 WHAT IS PRODUCTION MANAGEMENT?

THE FIRST NIGHT

They take their seat at the end of a row, notebook in hand, a few minutes before the start of the first performance. They may chat to a few of the audience sitting near them, possibly work colleagues. They will skim through the programme, starting at the back. Once the show starts, or even before, they make occasional notes. They are among the first people to leave the auditorium at the interval.

They return for the second half and continue to take notes. At the end of the show, they again leave quickly and disappear backstage or into the control room at the rear of the auditorium. There they talk to members of the production staff and promise to see them in the bar later.

This person is not the Director, the Writer or the Producer; he or she is the Production Manager – the person responsible for everything on stage that is not an actor!

So what does the description of their evening tell us about the production manager and their job? Let us look at it line by line.

'They take their seat at the end of a row'

This is because they may need to be able to leave the auditorium without causing a disturbance if something technical goes wrong during the performance.

'Notebook in hand'

They will want to take notes of anything that needs attending to before the next performance.

'A few minutes before the start of the first performance'

They don't want to miss the start of the show, as it is here that there may well be technical points to note. They may have been in the office up to now, possibly catching up on some paperwork that has not been done during the week.

'They may chat to a few of the audience sitting near them, possibly work colleagues'

A first night is an 'occasion' and the production manager will have made sure that their staff and guests have complimentary tickets (known as comps) to the show, probably sitting in a block.

'They will skim through the programme, starting at the back'

The staffing page and production credits will be at the back of the programme or playbill and, although they will have seen a proof of the programme, the production manager will be checking that everyone is included and that their names are spelt correctly.

'Once the show starts, or even before, they make occasional notes'

There will be specific cues or sequences that they will watch carefully, such as any that have proved difficult to get right or have had to be changed since the final dress rehearsal.

Cues and Sequences

A 'cue' (usually written as Q) is an instruction to a technician to carry out an action – to change the lighting, play a sound effect or move a piece of scenery.

A 'sequence' is a series of cues which happen together or one after the other – a scene change for example.

All cues are given by the Deputy Stage Manager working from the prompt script or 'book'.

As well as making notes about the technical aspects of the performance, this is an opportunity to reflect on how the production process has gone and also to note things which need doing for the next production which is probably about to start rehearsing.

'They are among the first people to leave the auditorium at the interval'

They know when the interval is. Although this is the first performance, they will have already seen the show through at least four or five times: once in the rehearsal room, at the Technical Rehearsal and at Dress Rehearsals. They will also have attended the read-through on the first day of rehearsals.

'They return for the second half and continue to take notes'

The interval will have been the opportunity to talk briefly to the director (and re-assure them) about how things are going and to make a quick visit backstage to make sure there are no problems.

Although there will have been dress rehearsals of the production, the audience are the final piece in the jigsaw puzzle. Their presence will definitely have an effect on the performers through nerves and extra adrenaline.

The director will be more interested than the production manager as to how an audience affects actors' performances. However the audience reaction (laughter and applause) may have an effect on the timing of technical moments. Their presence changes the acoustics of the auditorium (bodies absorb sound) and this will affect music and sound effects.

'At the end of the show, they again leave quickly and disappear backstage or into the control room at the rear of the auditorium. There they talk to members of the production staff and the promise to see them in the bar later.'

This is the most important part of this description of the evening – thanking people for their work. This is because any production manager is only as good as the people who will work for them and it is important to take the opportunity that a first night offers to make those people feel appreciated.

The Tech

The Technical Rehearsal (or Tech) is the point at which all aspects of a production are put together on stage for the first time. The show is worked through in sequence, getting every aspect right. A Tech can last for several days, or in the case of major West End or Broadway musicals, weeks.

Production Week

The time taken to rig, fit up, light and rehearse a show in the theatre may be a few hours, a few days or a few weeks. For ease of reference, throughout this book we will refer to this period as production week.

The first night is the culmination of a period of very intensive work while the show is prepared in the theatre – the Production Week – and this is preceded by a number of weeks of rehearsal, but the production manager's work will have started a long time before that.

If the production manager is part of a permanent organization, this first night will be just one in a season of productions. The production manager will have recruited the production staff (their team) for the season (some of them may be permanent members of staff) and will schedule their work throughout the season. The production manager's team consists of stage managers, electricians, technicians, sound engineers, set builders and painters, prop-makers and wardrobe staff.

During the production process the production manager will have worked closely with the director, the designers, the performers and administrators and office staff. They will have:

- Briefed the director and designers about the resources available for the production.
- Costed the production and kept a check on expenditure.
- Scheduled the work of each department and agreed any necessary overtime.
- Ensured that there is effective communication between everyone working on the production.
- Overseen the fit up and organized the best use of time during the production week.
- Ensured the safety of all concerned with the production and produced a risk assessment.
- Ensured that all technical moments work properly and that the director and designers are happy with the look of the show.

The Director's Overview

It is important to remember that the director will have the only overall view of the finished production; every team member, whether they are a manager, performer, or technician, is working towards the director's vision of how the production will work.

It is vital that the director is trusted by the rest of the team, who will only see individual parts of the whole picture, but also that the director trusts and allows individuals to do their job within the team.

A production manager will have had a number of years' experience working in technical theatre. They are likely to have worked their way up to Head of Department, perhaps moving from theatre to theatre for promotion and experience, and decided that they have the knowledge, experience and desire to run the whole production team.

A production manager needs to be able to do the following:

- Be flexible.
- Be objective.
- Carry out routine tasks quickly and efficiently.
- Communicate with a wide variety of personalities.
- Continue working well when tired.
- Deal with people's artistic temperaments.
- Delegate to others.
- Get onto people's wavelength.

- Have an overview.
- Keep up-to-date financial records.
- Lead from the front.
- Make lists.
- Manage people well.
- Plan ahead.
- Plan in detail.
- Praise others.
- Recruit and nurture appropriate staff.
- Remain calm.
- Resolve conflicts, be they artistic, financial, personality or inter-departmental.
- Run meetings.
- Show commitment to the production and organization.
- Solve problems.
- Think ahead.
- Think laterally.
- Trust others.
- Use computers and Information Technology as effective tools.
- Work on several projects at the same time.
- Work under pressure.
- Work with information accurately.

A production manager needs have an in-depth knowledge of the following:

- Costs
- Current theatre practice
- Employment legislation
- Where to contact experts and specialists
- Fire and licensing regulations
- Health and safety legislation and practice
- Likely future technical developments
- Skills needed by each department
- Suppliers (particularly of specialist materials)
- The technicalities of each department
- Basic engineering and construction
- Theatre terminology
- Details of the theatre building, stage, stock, equipment

- Union agreements
- What the team can achieve
- Whether technical moments are working or not
- Where to research things they don't know

Drama school training is beginning to become available for young, would-be production managers. Initial jobs would be as assistants, for which IT skills and a knowledge of the management of Health and Safety are essential. People who are coming to production management later in life will have learned a lot – both what to do and what not to do – from production managers they have worked for and will have their own ideas on how they want to do the job.

The individual nature of a production manager's job means that, to an extent, it can be tailored according to individual strengths, weaknesses and interests. The structure of the rest of the team can then be adjusted to make sure that there are no knowledge or skill gaps.

A production manager's job is to facilitate and co-ordinate the work of individual team members and departments. When it is done well the production team feel supported and appreciated and that they can concentrate on using their individual skills. When it is done badly, or not done at all, the production staff do not feel like a team and have to spend their time fighting their own corner, sorting out problems, finding information and cannot fully use the individual skills for which they were employed.

There is no one right way for production managers to work. This book describes how the job of production management can be approached, what the production manager needs to know and why, and what they need to do in order to 'make the show happen'.

2 WHO DOES WHAT IN THE THEATRE?

In this chapter we will look at the different structures of theatre organizations, how they are managed and staffed, and where the production manager fits into that structure.

AMATEUR THEATRE

Amateur theatre ranges from a group of friends who decide to get together to put on a single production, to a long-established company with several hundred members and their own theatre, who put on a number of productions every year. In some cases, amateur theatre members have the same job descriptions and responsibilities as in professional theatre, the only difference being that they are unpaid. Members may care to study how professional theatre operates and apply it to their own organization. The most important thing, in amateur as in professional theatre, is that everyone should know where their responsibilities begin and end, and have the knowledge, skills and support to carry them out.

TYPES OF PROFESSIONAL THEATRE ORGANIZATION

There are three main types of professional theatre organizations:
• presenting/receiving theatres
• producing theatres
• production companies
In this book we will be mainly concerned with the creation of new productions, which is done by producing theatres or production companies; but a production manager may also work in a presenting or receiving theatre.

Presenting /Receiving Theatres

• do not initiate their own productions;
• are unlikely to have a production manager;
• take in productions that have been rehearsed, built and performed at other, similar venues;
• take in productions that have been initiated by a production company for a specific venue (a West End or Broadway theatre, for example);
• have a small, permanent staff augmented by casuals;
• are usually funded modestly by the local council;
• with the exception of West End or Broadway theatres, run productions for a fixed period of time, often only a week;
• are likely to take in some larger-scale amateur productions.

Producing Theatres or Building-Based Companies

• initiate their own productions;
• are almost certain to have a permanent production manager;
• may enter into co-production deals so that their shows tour to other producing theatres or presenting/receiving houses;

- may take in productions from other producing theatres;
- have a large, permanent staff;
- are funded by local councils and the Arts Council;
- run productions for a fixed period of time, often four weeks, or operate a repertoire system;
- may take in some larger-scale amateur productions to augment their season, and as a service to the community.

Producing Companies

- initiate their own productions;
- rent theatres in which to mount their productions, or share the Box Office income with the theatre;
- will use permanent or freelance production managers;
- may enter into co-production deals so that they take over shows from producing theatres;
- have a very small, office-based staff augmented by freelance staff to work on productions;
- are hoping to run at a profit, but are underwritten by backers, known as 'angels';
- run productions for as long as possible so as to maximize their earnings;
- will not have any involvement with amateur productions.

Birmingham Repertory Theatre.

A Repertory Theatre Production Schedule			
January		**Main**	**Studio**
Monday	25	Dress Rehearsal	Studio Production Week
Tuesday	26 7.30pm	**The Dancing Years** (Amateur)	Studio Production Week
Wednesday	27 7.30pm	**The Dancing Years** (Amateur)	Studio Production Week
Thursday	28 7.30pm	**The Dancing Years** (Amateur)	7.45pm **Laurel & Hardy**
Friday	29 7.30pm	**The Dancing Years** (Amateur)	7.45pm **Laurel & Hardy**
Saturday	30 7.30pm	**The Dancing Years** (Amateur)	7.45pm **Laurel & Hardy**
February			
Monday	1	Dress Rehearsal	7.45pm **Laurel & Hardy**
Tuesday	2 7.30pm	**Lock Up Your Daughters** (Amateur)	7.45pm **Laurel & Hardy**
Wednesday	3 7.30pm	**Lock Up Your Daughters** (Amateur)	7.45pm **Laurel & Hardy**
Thursday	4 7.30pm	**Lock Up Your Daughters** (Amateur)	7.45pm **Laurel & Hardy**
Friday	5 7.30pm	**Lock Up Your Daughters** (Amateur)	7.45pm **Laurel & Hardy**
Saturday	6 2.30pm	**Lock Up Your Daughters** (Amateur)	
	7.30pm	**Lock Up Your Daughters** (Amateur)	7.45pm **Laurel & Hardy**
Monday	8	Production Week	7.45pm **Laurel & Hardy**
Tuesday	9	Production Week	7.45pm **Laurel & Hardy**
Wednesday	10	Production Week	7.45pm **Laurel & Hardy**
Thursday	11	Production Week	7.45pm **Laurel & Hardy**
Friday	12 8.00pm	**A Chorus of Disapproval**	7.45pm **Laurel & Hardy**
Saturday	13 8.00pm	**A Chorus of Disapproval**	7.45pm **Laurel & Hardy**
Monday	15 7.30pm	**A Chorus of Disapproval**	7.45pm **Laurel & Hardy**
Tuesday	16 7.30pm	**A Chorus of Disapproval**	7.45pm **Laurel & Hardy**
Wednesday	17 7.30pm	**A Chorus of Disapproval**	7.45pm **Laurel & Hardy**
Thursday	18 7.30pm	**A Chorus of Disapproval**	7.45pm **Laurel & Hardy**
Friday	19 8.00pm	**A Chorus of Disapproval**	7.45pm **Laurel & Hardy**
Saturday	20 8.00pm	**A Chorus of Disapproval**	7.45pm **Laurel & Hardy**
Monday	22 7.30pm	**A Chorus of Disapproval**	7.45pm Dress Rehearsal
Tuesday	23 7.30pm	**A Chorus of Disapproval**	7.45pm **Dido Queen of Carthage** (Amateur)
Wednesday	24 7.30pm	**A Chorus of Disapproval**	7.45pm **Dido Queen of Carthage** (Amateur)
Thursday	25 7.30pm	**A Chorus of Disapproval**	7.45pm **Dido Queen of Carthage** (Amateur)
Friday	26 7.30pm	**A Chorus of Disapproval**	7.45pm **Dido Queen of Carthage** (Amateur)
Saturday	27 2.30pm	**A Chorus of Disapproval**	
	8.00pm	**A Chorus of Disapproval**	7.45pm **Dido Queen of Carthage** (Amateur)

Types of Producing Theatre

There are three systems under which producing theatres operate:

- repertory
- repertoire
- stagione

Repertory Theatres

- are usually known as 'regional reps'
- have a season of plays in which productions are staged one after another;
- perform each production every night (except Sundays) for a limited run, often four weeks;

A Repertory Theatre Production Schedule (continued)					
March					
Monday	1	7.30pm	A Chorus of Disapproval	7.45pm	Dress Rehearsal
Tuesday	2	7.30pm	A Chorus of Disapproval	7.45pm	**Dido Queen of Carthage** (Amateur)
Wednesday	3	7.30pm	A Chorus of Disapproval	7.45pm	**Dido Queen of Carthage** (Amateur)
Thursday	4	7.30pm	A Chorus of Disapproval	7.45pm	**Dido Queen of Carthage** (Amateur)
Friday	5	7.30pm	A Chorus of Disapproval	7.45pm	**Dido Queen of Carthage** (Amateur)
Saturday	6	2.30pm	A Chorus of Disapproval		
		8.00pm	A Chorus of Disapproval	7.45pm	**Dido Queen of Carthage** (Amateur)
Monday	8	7.30pm	A Chorus of Disapproval		
Tuesday	9	7.30pm	A Chorus of Disapproval		
Wednesday	10	7.30pm	A Chorus of Disapproval		
Thursday	11	7.30pm	A Chorus of Disapproval		
Friday	12	8.00pm	A Chorus of Disapproval		
Saturday	13	8.00pm	A Chorus of Disapproval		
Monday	15		Production Week		
Tuesday	16		Production Week		
Wednesday	17		Production Week		
Thursday	18		Production Week		
Friday	19		Production Week		
Saturday	20	8.00pm	**Little Shop of Horrors**		
Monday	22	7.30pm	**Little Shop of Horrors**		
Tuesday	23	7.30pm	**Little Shop of Horrors**		
Wednesday	24	7.30pm	**Little Shop of Horrors**		
Thursday	25	7.30pm	**Little Shop of Horrors**		
Friday	26	8.00pm	**Little Shop of Horrors**		
Saturday	27	2.30pm	**Little Shop of Horrors**		
		8.00pm	**Little Shop of Horrors**		

- start rehearsing the next production as soon as the previous one has opened;
- encourage audiences to 'subscribe' to the season, and to see all the productions over the course of several months;
- may also operate a Studio Theatre.

Repertoire Houses

- mostly comprise the big national companies;
- have seasons of plays in which a number of productions alternate with each other;
- have each production in the repertoire for a number of months, but perform it for only a few days at a time;

- rehearse several productions at once, and open them in fairly quick succession;
- encourage audiences to see a number of productions in a short period of time (this is particularly attractive to tourists);
- usually have more than one auditorium.

Stagione

- are mostly used by Opera Houses who wish to attract international stars;
- are similar to repertoire;
- have a season with only a small number of productions available at any one time;
- rotate productions so that each production

has a break of at least one night between performances (to protect singers' voices);
• keep productions in the repertoire for a number of years, but re-cast and re-rehearse them for each season.

THEATRE ADMINISTRATION

In order to understand who does what in the theatre it is important to understand how theatre organizations are structured. Much of the running of a theatre is finance driven, and this is usually reflected in the organizational structure.

A producing theatre's income can be divided into two parts: income earned through the box office, and unearned income in the form of grants. Its expenditure is, to a large extent, fixed whatever shows are produced. Because it has a large, permanent staff to pay, and a building which it must heat, light, maintain and perhaps pay rent and rates on, nearly two thirds of each year's budget may already be accounted for before any production is mounted.

Arts Councils	

In the UK there are separate Arts Councils for England, Wales, Scotland and Northern Ireland.

They 'develop, sustain and promote' the arts by distributing public money from government and the national lottery to artists and arts organizations.

The Business Plan

As we will see when we look at the production process, all theatre is a dictatorship – though hopefully a benevolent one – but it is also a business. Everyone working in a theatre should be supporting the vision of the artistic

A Repertoire Performance Schedule

January

Monday	25		Production Week
Tuesday	26		Production Week
Wednesday	27	7.30pm	The Recruiting Officer (Preview)
Thursday	28	7.30pm	The Recruiting Officer (Preview)
Friday	29	7.30pm	The Recruiting Officer (First Night)
Saturday	30	2.30pm	The Recruiting Officer
		7.30pm	The Recruiting Officer

February

Monday	1	7.30pm	The Recruiting Officer
Tuesday	2	7.00pm	The Recruiting Officer (Press Night)
Wednesday	3	7.30pm	The Recruiting Officer
Thursday	4	2.30pm	The Recruiting Officer
		7.30pm	The Recruiting Officer
Friday	5	7.30pm	The Recruiting Officer
Saturday	6	2.30pm	The Recruiting Officer
		7.30pm	The Recruiting Officer
Monday	8		Production Week
Tuesday	9		Production Week
Wednesday	10	7.30pm	Heartbreak House (Preview)
Thursday	11	7.30pm	Heartbreak House (Preview)
Friday	12	7.30pm	Heartbreak House
Saturday	13	2.30pm	Heartbreak House
		7.30pm	Heartbreak House
Monday	15	7.30pm	Heartbreak House
Tuesday	16	7.00pm	Heartbreak House (Press Night)
Wednesday	17	7.30pm	The Recruiting Officer
Thursday	18	2.30pm	The Recruiting Officer
		7.30pm	The Recruiting Officer
Friday	19	7.30pm	Heartbreak House
Saturday	20	2.30pm	Heartbreak House
		7.30pm	Heartbreak House
Monday	22	7.30pm	Heartbreak House
Tuesday	23	7.30pm	Heartbreak House
Wednesday	24	7.30pm	Heartbreak House
Thursday	25	2.30pm	Heartbreak House
		7.30pm	Heartbreak House
Friday	26	7.30pm	The Recruiting Officer
Saturday	27	2.30pm	The Recruiting Officer
		7.30pm	The Recruiting Officer

See page 13

OPPOSITE: *The Royal National Theatre.*

March			
Monday	1	7.30pm	**The Recruiting Officer**
Tuesday	2	7.30pm	**Heartbreak House**
Wednesday	3	7.30pm	**Heartbreak House**
Thursday	4	2.30pm	**Heartbreak House**
		7.30pm	**The Recruiting Officer**
Friday	5	7.30pm	**The Recruiting Officer**
Saturday	6	2.30pm	**The Recruiting Officer**
		7.30pm	**Heartbreak House**
Monday	8		Production Week
Tuesday	9		Production Week
Wednesday	10	7.30pm	**Family Reunion** (Preview)
Thursday	11	7.30pm	**Family Reunion** (Preview)
Friday	12	7.30pm	**Family Reunion** (First Night)
Saturday	13	2.30pm	**Family Reunion**
		7.30pm	**Family Reunion**
Monday	15	7.30pm	**Family Reunion**
Tuesday	16	7.00pm	**Family Reunion** (Press Night)
Wednesday	17	7.30pm	**Heartbreak House**
Thursday	18	2.30pm	**Heartbreak House**
		7.30pm	**Heartbreak House**
Friday	19	7.30pm	**Family Reunion**
Saturday	20	2.30pm	**Family Reunion**
		7.30pm	**Family Reunion**

director – but at the same time they should also be aware of their financial responsibilities or budgets. It is vitally important therefore that the vision and budgets are clearly expressed and understood by the whole team – for theatre is very much a team sport!

The artistic vision and how it will be achieved is usually described in the business plan. This is a large document that should be

A SWOT Analysis

This assesses and records the current strengths and weaknesses of an organization or department, and looks at future opportunities for and threats to them. It can be helpful in determining and prioritizing action that needs to be taken, by the organization or individuals.

The Royal Opera House, Covent Garden.

revised every year by the board and senior management team. It will start with the aims and goals of the theatre (often called the 'mission statement'), and will go on to describe the practicalities of how the theatre intends to achieve those aims and goals in the coming year. It will look back on the successes and failures of the previous year, and it may well contain a SWOT analysis of all the different areas of the organization.

A business plan may sound very boring and full of management speak, but it should be a working document that influences and supports every management and policy decision made.

The Board of Directors

Most theatres are governed by a board of directors. This can have between five and twenty-five members, and will be made up of:

An Opera Season Schedule

January

Monday	25		Rehearsals Das Rhinegold
Tuesday	26		Rehearsals Nabucco
Wednesday	27		Rehearsals Das Rhinegold
Thursday	28		Rehearsals Nabucco
Friday	29	7.30pm	**Das Rhinegold** (First Night)
Saturday	30	7.30pm	**Nabucco** (First Night)

February

Monday	1		Rehearsals Cunning Little Vixen
Tuesday	2	7.30pm	**Das Rhinegold**
Wednesday	3	7.30pm	**Nabucco**
Thursday	4		Rehearsals Cunning Little Vixen
Friday	5	7.30pm	**Das Rhinegold**
Saturday	6	7.30pm	**Nabucco**
Monday	8	7.30pm	**Nabucco**
Tuesday	9	7.30pm	**Das Rhinegold** (Last Night)
Wednesday	10	7.30pm	**Cunning Little Vixen** (First Night)
Thursday	11		Rehearsals Carmen
Friday	12	7.30pm	**Nabucco**
Saturday	13	7.30pm	**Cunning Little Vixen**
Monday	15		Rehearsals Carmen
Tuesday	16		Rehearsals Carmen
Wednesday	17	2.30pm	**Cunning Little Vixen**
Thursday	18	2.30pm	**Nabucco**
Friday	19	7.30pm	**Cunning Little Vixen**
Saturday	20	7.30pm	**Nabucco**
Monday	22	7.30pm	**Nabucco**
Tuesday	23	7.30pm	**Carmen** (First Night)
Wednesday	24	2.30pm	**Cunning Little Vixen**
Thursday	25	7.30pm	**Carmen**
Friday	26	7.30pm	**Nabucco** (Last Night)
Saturday	27	7.30pm	**Carmen**

March

Monday	1		Rehearsals Puccini's Trittico
Tuesday	2		Rehearsals Puccini's Trittico
Wednesday	3	7.30pm	**Cunning Little Vixen**
Thursday	4	7.30pm	**Carmen**
Friday	5	7.30pm	**Cunning Little Vixen** (Last Night)
Saturday	6	7.30pm	**Carmen**
Monday	8		Rehearsals Puccini's Trittico
Tuesday	9	7.30pm	**Carmen**
Wednesday	10	7.30pm	**Carmen**
Thursday	11	7.30pm	**Puccini's Trittico** (First Night)
Friday	12	7.30pm	**Carmen**
Saturday	13	7.30pm	**Puccini's Trittico**
Monday	15		Rehearsals Barber of Seville
Tuesday	16	7.00pm	**Carmen**
Wednesday	17	7.30pm	**Puccini's Trittico**
Thursday	18	7.30pm	**Carmen**
Friday	19	7.30pm	**Puccini's Trittico**
Saturday	20	7.30pm	**Carmen**
Monday	22	7.30pm	**Carmen**
Tuesday	23	7.00pm	**Puccini's Trittico**
Wednesday	24	7.30pm	**Barber of Seville** (First Night)
Thursday	25	7.30pm	**Carmen**
Friday	26	7.30pm	**Puccini's Trittico**
Saturday	27	7.30pm	**Barber of Seville**

See page 13

This board will have little to do with the day-to-day running of the theatre, but will meet every two months or so to consider the major issues affecting the theatre, in particular the overall financial situation and the choice of productions. The day-to-day running is left to the chief executive and the artistic director, whom the board appoint, and the heads of each area of the organization; together these are often known as the **senior management team**.

The Chief Executive and Artistic Director

The **Chief Executive** is usually the senior member of the administration staff, sometimes called the General Manager or the Administrator. He or she is responsible for strategic and financial planning and control, the general running of the theatre, and the appointment of the

- representatives of the funding bodies (to look after the interests of the taxpayers);
- representatives of the local community (because of their local knowledge and influence, and for specialist skills);
- the chief executive and artistic director (as the senior 'officers' of the theatre);
- a number of experienced theatre practitioners (for their knowledge of the industry and to support the 'artistic vision').

A Budget Breakdown for a Repertory Season		
Budget Area	**Detail**	**Share of Annual Budget**
Production Based Income	Box office Sponsorship Program sales Co-productions	53%
Fixed Income	Arts Council grant Local Council grants	47%
Fixed Expenditure	Staff salaries Heating Lighting Rent Rates Maintenance	62%
Production Expenditure See page 14	Actors salaries (including subsistence, travel and holiday pay) Musicians salaries Creative team fees (including expenses and travel) Production budgets Overtime Casuals and freelancers Marketing Royalties	38%

senior management team. They need to have excellent management and administration skills and experience, but also a flexibility of approach that will support the artistic vision.

The **Artistic Director** is responsible for choosing the productions that the theatre will mount, and for directing a number of them. It is not possible for one person to direct a whole season of productions, and therefore the artistic director is responsible for appointing an Associate Director, who would be a permanent member of staff, or Guest Directors, who would be engaged to direct one production on a freelance basis.

An artistic director needs to be an experienced director of a wide range of productions. He or she will have the additional vision, imagination, planning and communication skills to prog-

ramme and 'sell' to the board, the senior management team, staff and audience a whole season of productions. This must be balanced in terms of style and content, and achievable in terms of budget (income and expenditure), schedule and staff. The artistic director will build or maintain an identity for the theatre, and work closely with the marketing department in projecting this identity to the public.

An artistic director will usually have had a university or drama school education, and may have worked as an actor and or sometimes as a stage manager before starting to direct. They may have received a bursary to work in a regional theatre for a year and will have started as a freelance director before, perhaps, becoming an associate and then making the step – and it is a big step – to artistic director.

The pressures of being a senior manager of an organization as well as directing productions should not be underestimated. In some theatre structures the artistic director is contracted as the chief executive or joint chief executive; however, this can lead to conflict between the artistic and financial sides of the organization.

The Senior Management Team

This team will meet formally at least once a week, and its members are responsible for running the different areas of the theatre. They will each have their own budgets or income targets to achieve, and will be responsible for employing and managing staff. The membership of the senior management team will vary according to the structure of the theatre, but will usually consist of the chief executive, the artistic director, the production manager, the marketing manager, the theatre manager and the finance director.

The **marketing manager** is usually responsible for publicity and sales. He or she will run the publicity and press office, and the box office team. Their staff are responsible for all posters, brochures, programmes and press coverage, and for selling tickets to the public. Most theatres run a subscription scheme to encourage people to visit the theatre regularly. The marketing department uses the box office computer not only to allocate seats and produce tickets, but also to gather information about customers, which is used to target future publicity and sales and to produce statistics.

The **theatre manager** is responsible for the public face of the theatre; this will include front-of-house staff, security staff, maintenance and cleaning. They will also have a close involvement with the operation of the bars and restaurant, although these may be run by a separate company.

The **finance director**, as the title suggests, is responsible for the day-to-day finances of the theatre. This includes the payment of salaries, fees and invoices; banking money taken by the box office or catering; dealing with petty cash; and producing regular financial reports for the board of directors and the senior management team, so they can keep track of the budgets for which they are responsible. The chart on page 20 summarizes the staffing structure of a producing theatre.

CREATIVE TEAMS

As part of their contract, the artistic director will direct a number of productions in each season. The remaining productions will be the responsibility of associate or guest directors, chosen by the artistic director.

In consultation with the artistic director and the production manager, each director will engage the rest of the creative team. This will consist of the designer, who is usually responsible for both the set and the costumes; the lighting

---

This theatre aims to provide for the people of this city and beyond, a high quality, well balanced programme of local, national and international theatre.

We will create and produce theatre that:

➤   inspires, absorbs and delights

➤   engages an audience intellectually and emotionally

➤   celebrates the uniqueness of the live event

➤   tells stories relevant to today

➤   is imaginative and entertaining

An example of a mission statement.

19

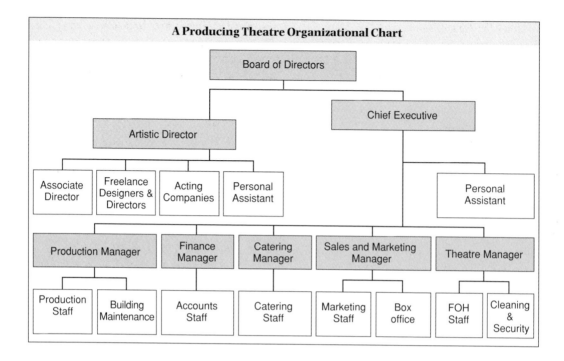

A Producing Theatre Organizational Chart

designer; and the sound designer. Depending on the requirements of the production there may also be a musical director, a choreographer, a fight director, and a voice or dialect coach.

Choosing the Cast

The director will also choose the cast for the production either from actors they know and have worked with before, or by holding auditions. Again this is usually done in conjunction with the artistic director. Pictures and brief details about actors can be found in casting directories and on websites world-wide. Directors will study these, and look at submissions from agents in order to decide whom they want to audition. In England the majority of actors are based in London, so that is where auditions usually take place – often at the offices of *Spotlight* who also happen to publish the main casting directory. For actors who are based more locally, directors may also hold auditions at their base theatre.

Freelancers

Most designers work on a freelance basis. This means that they:
- will not be employees of the theatre
- will be paid a fee for their work
- may also receive a small percentage of the box office income
- are classed as 'self-employed' and look after their own tax affairs
- are probably represented by an agent who, for a percentage of their fees, negotiates on their behalf
- generally have to be working on more than one production at once, due to the size of fees paid
- may not be available on a full-time basis to any one production. You should note days when designers are committed elsewhere (their non-availability)

The Set Designer

The set designer is responsible for how a production will look. He or she will produce a 1:25 scale model of the set, and scale drawings of the set on the stage (the groundplan), and drawings of each piece of scenery.

They are usually also responsible for the look of furniture and props, and will produce lists of these, together with references, drawings or model pieces where needed.

Designers must be excellent communicators. They must also be able to combine artistry with practicality, because however good a set design may look, it will not serve the production if it is dangerous for the actors, exceeds the budget, or cannot be built safely in the time available. They also need to have an extensive knowledge of historical periods, and to be able to sketch and to draw accurate technical drawings. They must understand the way in which production departments work, and the technicalities of how scenery and props are made.

A designer will probably have trained at an art school or taken a specialist theatre design course. They may well have started their career working as a prop-maker, scenic artist or carpenter and may also have worked as a model maker or assistant to a more established designer.

The Costume Designer

Quite often, for budgetary reasons, the same person will be asked to design both the set and the costumes; it is only the larger companies that can afford separate designers.

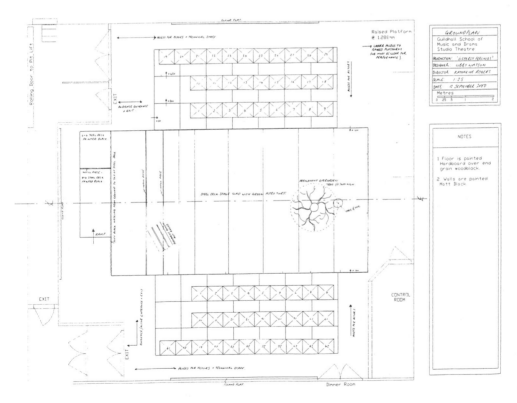

A studio groundplan showing seating as well as the set. Designer: Libby Watson

A costume design. Designer: Jan Bee Brown

When responsible for costumes, the designer again has to have extensive period and technical knowledge, must be able to produce accurate and informative drawings, and must work well with members of the costume department and the performers.

Often the director will have a designer with whom they feel they work particularly well. This will be based on good communication and trust, probably built up over a number of years.

We will look much more closely at the work of designers and their relationship with the production manager when we discuss the pre-production process in a later chapter.

The Lighting Designer

The lighting designer is responsible for making sure that the performers can be seen (or occasionally not seen) as required, and that the production looks as good as it possibly can.

Lighting is used to convey important information about the piece, which cannot necessarily be conveyed by the set design – for instance the time of day, the season or the

Designers' Contracts

In the UK, Equity is the union that represents designers; in America it is the United Scenic Artists.

There are standard union contracts for designers, or a theatre or production company may have their own standard contract. These will lay out terms and conditions, and state how the designer will be paid. This is usually in three phases:
• on signing the contract
• on producing completed designs (drawings and model)
• on the opening night of the production
The designer will also be entitled to model and travel expenses, accommodation and a biography in the programme.

It should be part of the terms of their contract that designers are totally available once the show moves into the theatre.

Dramatic lighting for a production. Lighting Designer: Matt Eagland. Photo: Laurence Burns

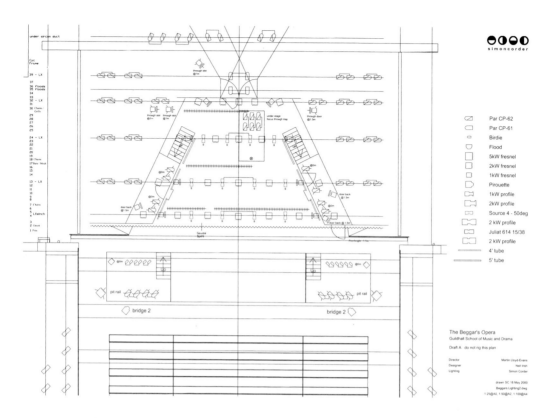

A computer-drawn lighting plan. Lighting Designer: Simon Corder.

weather – and for setting the mood of the scene and heightening tension. It can be used to concentrate the audience's attention on one part of the stage or one performer, and it may also be used, particularly in musicals, as an entertainment in its own right.

The lighting designer has an increasingly wide range of technology at his or her disposal and needs to be able to use this in a creative and artistic way to contribute to the production. Ideally they will be involved in the creative process from very early on. They will have discussions with the director and designer, but unless it is a major West End or Broadway production, will not have to produce the lighting plan until near the end of rehearsals.

Lighting designers need to be able to work well under pressure. Unlike set designers they cannot look at a model version of their design (except in fairly crude terms), and they have only a very limited time once the show comes into the theatre in which to turn their concept into reality.

A lighting designer will usually have started as an electrician (although there are some specialist lighting design courses) and started to light productions in the theatre where they are a member of staff, before becoming freelance. It is sometimes part of the chief electrician's job description to light a number of productions in a season.

The Sound Designer

Sound can be used in similar ways to lighting to give information to an audience about the scene and mood, and particularly to support the work of performers in building tension in a scene. By the choice of music before a show even starts, messages can be given to the audience about the type of entertainment they are to experience.

The sound designer must work particularly closely with the director. There is no point in them following their own ideas about a piece and producing lots of music and effects, only to find out that the director is interpreting the play in an entirely different way.

Usually the 'design' aspect of their work has more to do with the choice, placement and use of equipment, and how – indeed, if – musicians and singers are to be amplified. Having said that, the sound designer will need to be very creative in acquiring sound effects, and sensitive in the way in which music is used.

The sound designer is the member of the creative team most likely to be on the theatre

A sound mixer.

staff. He or she may also be responsible for operating sound for the show, although this is not an ideal situation, as they really need to be able to concentrate on the effectiveness of sound in the production as a whole, rather than on the practicality of operating the sound system.

Sound is probably the department in technical theatre that is developing most quickly in terms of technology. Computers are often used to create, store and replay sound, and to take over the technicalities of operating a show so that the sound technician can concentrate on balancing the final sound. The days of using tape and cassette are almost over, and mini disk and recordable CD are now used, or the sound may be stored digitally in a sampler, PC or laptop.

The sound designer will probably have started their career as a junior member of a sound or even electrics department before specializing and becoming freelance, or joining a specialist sound company. In addition to a complete understanding of the technology, a sound designer's most important tool is their ears.

The Musical Director

The musical director (or MD) is the person in charge of music on a production. He or she is responsible for teaching the music and harmonies to performers in rehearsals, and will usually conduct the orchestra or play the piano at performances. In opera they will be known as the 'conductor', or 'maestro', and will be supported by a music staff that includes *repetiteurs*, who play the piano for rehearsals. In conjunction with administrative staff, the MD will select and contract members of the orchestra, and rehearse them separately from the cast. In theatre, as opposed to opera, the orchestra is usually known as the band. Hence rehearsals with or for the band will be known as 'band calls', and their dressing room as the 'band room'.

25

The MD will work closely with the director and choreographer throughout rehearsals, and, if it is an opera or a musical, will have been involved in auditioning performers. They will also have to have a good relationship with the sound designer and operator to ensure that the music is heard at its best in performance. On some productions, particularly dramas, the MD may also be asked to compose or arrange music for the production. They may well have to produce or alter band parts for the orchestra.

Musical directors will have trained as professional musicians, and will probably have worked their way up, starting by playing in orchestras for shows, and gradually taking on more responsibility. They will almost certainly be expert pianists, and will play the piano for auditions and rehearsals. In performance they are likely to play an electronic keyboard, which can reproduce any sound from a full orchestra to an individual instrument, or any noise that has been recorded digitally (known as a sample).

The Choreographer

This person, usually a dancer or ex-dancer, is responsible for inventing and teaching to the performers all movement during musical numbers. Again they will work closely with the director and musical director, and will have been involved in choosing the performers at auditions. Once a show opens, they will move on to another production and will rely on the dance captain – an experienced member of the cast – to keep the choreography up to scratch, to rehearse understudies, and to take physical warm-ups.

Physical and vocal warm-ups need to happen before each performance. If they are to happen on stage, technical departments will need to

This fight needed close collaboration between the fight director, the performer, wardrobe and props. Photo: Marion Marrs

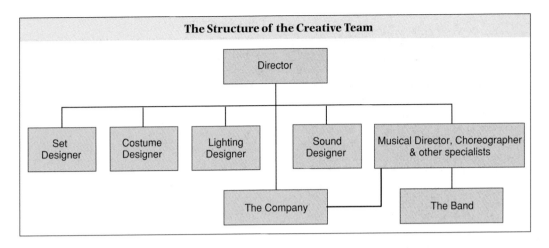

The Structure of the Creative Team

know, as it will affect when they can check and set up for the show.

The Fight Director

This is a highly specialized member of the creative team, and he or she will be engaged – indeed it is an Equity rule that they must be –

A Fight

Equity – the actors' and stage managers' union defines a fight as 'a specialized performance involving two or more people using fists, implements or weapons, which requires choreography and supervision for safety.'

It requires the management to provide personal accident insurance for those taking part in a fight.

A stage fight must always be rehearsed on stage in the correct lighting state just before each performance to ensure that the performers remember the moves exactly.

This needs scheduling so that nothing else is going onstage at the same time.

if a production contains a fight. They may well be a performer in their own right, but will have had specialist training in combat and weapons. It is their job to make sure that a fight is effective but also safe. There are many tricks that can be used on stage to assist with this. Close liaison with the designer, wardrobe and props departments are often necessary.

The fight director will probably only be engaged for a few sessions. They will set the fight early in rehearsals, attend a few rehearsals to tidy it up, and (importantly) be in attendance the first time the fight is rehearsed in the actual set, and at a dress rehearsal.

The Voice or Dialect Coach

Also specialists – and there are very few of them – **voice coaches** are experts on the correct use of the voice and in making sure that performers can be heard. They will have been an important part of an actor's training, and are used, particularly by the bigger companies, to ensure the continued correct use of the actor's instrument.

Dialect coaches are used where a show requires regional or foreign accents. It is important that all members of the cast speak with the same accent if they are supposed to be from the same location, so dialect coaches will

> ## The Production Office
>
> The production manager's base is a busy place. The phone is always ringing, and there is usually a queue of people waiting to check or discuss some aspect of the current production or a future one, or bringing a problem that needs solving.
>
> It is important that the production manager is as available as possible at all times, and is ready to make decisions quickly, as any delay can have a knock-on effect to all other departments.
>
> To facilitate this, the production office should be geared up to doing the routine tasks as quickly as possible. There are plenty of these, many of them to do with finance, such as petty cash, orders, timesheets, contracts.

come to rehearsals and teach the actors exactly how regional or foreign accents are produced. They will also leave tapes for actors to practise with. They will attend dress rehearsals, give notes afterwards, and may revisit the show during its run to ensure the play or individuals in it have not moved location.

Performers

This book does not attempt to discuss the work of performers in amateur or professional theatre, except where a production manager deals with them directly. This will be mostly in the area of ensuring their safety, and making sure that everything is in place to enable them to do their job.

Certain members of the production manager's team will, of course, have a lot to do with the performers. As we will see later, this particularly includes stage management and wardrobe.

PRODUCTION MANAGEMENT

We have looked briefly at the job of production manager in the first chapter, but it is important to understand where they fit into the structure of a theatre or theatre organization. As we can see from this chapter, they are a member of the senior management team and are responsible for all the technical and staffing aspects of productions, especially budgeting, scheduling and safety. They may have a production assistant to undertake some of the routine work, and a production secretary to help run the production office.

3 THE PRODUCTION MANAGER'S TEAM

A team can be defined as a group of individuals working together and separately towards a common objective, and this is very much the case in theatre. There can be few clearer objectives than the first performance of a production, and while each department and individual will have their own responsibilities, they need to be in constant communication about each other's needs.

The structure of the production team will be different in every theatre organization, but it will nearly always be led by the production manager.

There are likely to be the following departments – although depending on the organization, some may be amalgamated, some will not exist, and others split into more than one department:

- stage management
- stage technicians
- scenic construction
- scene-painting
- prop-making
- electrics
- sound
- wardrobe

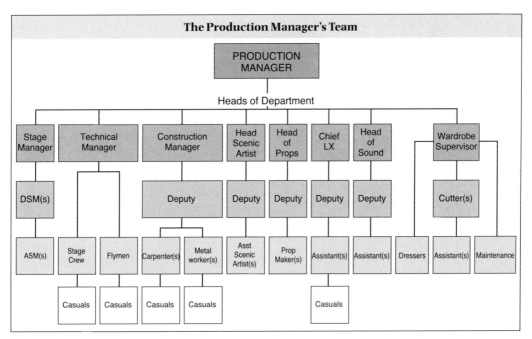

The Production Manager's Team

Each department will have a supervisor or chief, and these people are generally known as **heads of department** (HODs). They are the production manager's key allies, and when the team is working well, in addition to running their departments as teams, HODs will work together as a team.

In conjunction with the production manager, HODs will be responsible for recruiting their department members to agreed staffing and skill levels. They will be responsible to the production manager for the day-to-day running of their department, and will be expected to do this safely and efficiently within agreed budgets and deadlines. Daily management responsibilities for HODs include:

- working out when members of the department are required to work (their calls);
- deciding what each person does when they are working;

- ensuring the standard to which they carry out that work;
- sourcing and ordering the materials their department needs in order to do its work;
- making sure that the department keeps its working areas clean and tidy.

Importantly, to ensure that their staff get paid, the HOD will check and sign departmental time sheets before passing them on to production management. They will also keep their staff informed about the productions being worked on and what future plans the theatre has. Where appropriate, they will try and arrange training to advance the skills of their staff.

RECRUITMENT, INDUCTION AND APPRAISAL

A production manager will be responsible for recruiting their team, and needs to acquire skills in drafting job descriptions, and in interviewing and appraising staff. In the UK, nearly all jobs for production staff are advertised in *The Stage*, which is the industry's weekly trade newspaper. The equivalents in America are *Backstage*, *Show Business* and *Variety*.

In addition there are places where people seeking work can advertise, notably the Stage Management Association's freelist. However, theatre is a relatively small industry, and word of mouth plays a big part in recruitment. All theatre people need to be good at networking and to remember that they are only as good as their last job.

A **job description** (*see* page 32) is the basis of all employment, and should reflect what the employee is expected to do. It should state the job purpose, to whom and for whom the employee is responsible, and the main duties. It should refer to the way in which the employee is expected to work, and the terms of employment such as salary, overtime arrangements, probation period and length of notice.

Trusting Your Staff

As already discussed in the first chapter, a production manager is only as good as the staff who will work for them, and you should trust those staff to work conscientiously for you and to the best of their ability.

You should leave your HODs to run their departments in their own way, although you will want to ensure a unified style when it comes to communication (both internal and external).

You will also expect your HODs to support you by sticking to both the budget and schedule, and to talk to you as soon as they envisage any problems over either of these.

You will want to make sure that HODs share your high standards in all their work but especially when it comes to working safely.

The advertisement should state the job title, a summary of the duties, what is being looked for in terms of experience and training, the salary, the closing date for applications, and the starting date. Each candidate should be sent a pack consisting of:

- the job description;
- the candidate specification, which should list the essential or desirable experience, training and qualities you are looking for;
- an introduction to the theatre and department, stating the type of work done and the facilities available;
- a list of current staff;
- an application form (which applicants should fill in fully, and *not* put ' refer to enclosed CV');
- an indication of when and where interviews will be held.

The production manager should not interview candidates on their own, but should get together an interview panel. Who this includes will depend on the post being filled, but both sexes should be represented. The panel should select interviewees based on the candidate specification, and should draw up a standard list of questions which each candidate is asked. The interview questions should refer to the terms of the job description, and should give the candidate an opportunity to say how their experience qualifies them for the job. The interview process should include a tour of the theatre, and an opportunity to meet other members of the department and to ask questions of them and of the interview panel. Depending on the level of the appointment, it may be appropriate to ask candidates to complete a practical or written test or to make a presentation to the interview panel.

The final decision on whom to employ should be based on the interview, but also the candidate specification. An unsuccessful interviewee is entitled to challenge a decision if

---

References

Application forms will always ask for two referees, though permission should be sought before approaching them.

It is also common practice to approach production managers, HODs or designers with whom the candidate has worked, and who may be better known to you than the formal referees.

Referees are legally bound to give a good account of the candidate, and you should bear this in mind when you take up references – be prepared to 'read between the lines' – and also if you are asked to be a referee.

---

they meet all the criteria, and the production manager needs to be able to give a good reason why they chose one applicant and not another.

When a new member of staff starts there should be a formal induction process. This should include:

- a full tour of the building(s);
- an explanation of everything the new employee needs to know about how the organization functions;
- an introduction to all members of staff, especially those with whom they will be working directly;
- being issued with, and then signing for, all health and safety information and equipment;
- having training arranged if necessary;
- dealing with any financial or contract matters;
- setting up their IT provision.

There should be regular reviews of a new employee's progress. This should be documented, and should again refer back to the job

Job Description Construction Manager

Job purpose
As a Head of Department, to be responsible for the manufacture and delivery of scenery and related items for productions in the Main House, the Studio and at other theatres on tour, and for running the Scenic Workshop.

Responsible to: Production Manager
Responsible for: Scenic Workshop staff
                Freelance and Casual construction staff.

Main duties
- costing the work of the department in terms of time and materials.
- in conjunction with other departments, scheduling the work of the department in terms of time, space and personnel.
- ordering materials as required for the work.
- manufacturing the scenery or related items within the agreed schedule and budget.
- overseeing the fitting up of the scenic elements of all productions within the agreed time.
- ensuring that all scenery items are ready for use at the relevant time in production week.
- maintaining the scenery and related items of the show in performance and carrying out regular safety checks where necessary.
- altering stock items of scenery as necessary.
- undertaking ordering of materials needed for the work.
- ensuring that the scenic workshop and other areas the department may be using are kept clean and tidy and that all workshop equipment and equipment used on stage is looked after and properly and regularly maintained.
- overall responsibility for the scenery store.
- such other duties as may reasonably be required from time to time from a Head of Department within a regional Repertory Theatre.

In connection with the above, the construction manager will:
- discuss the designs (working drawings and scale models) with the designer, advise and agree on suitable or in-house construction techniques and interpret the designs to the designer's satisfaction.
- carry out research and development where necessary.
- liaise with other production departments about what is required of items of scenery and schedule the work of the scenic workshop in conjunction with those departments.
- hold costing/scheduling meetings with the rest of the department and where necessary, the scenic artist.
- devise and maintain suitable systems for the physical and paperwork control of items bought in bulk.
- keep records of materials ordered and expenditure on productions.
- decide what items are kept in the scenery store and ensure that an up to date record of its contents is made and maintained and that the store is kept tidy.
- be expected to work on stage during fit ups and strikes and production weeks.
- advise show staff using scenic items how they are intended to be used and attend parts of the technical rehearsal to ensure that the elements are used correctly.
- attend a dress rehearsal of each production.
- be line manager for the scenic workshop staff and supervise their work and that of other members of staff, including casuals, who may be delegated to the department.
- be aware of and observe the theatre's Health and Safety policy and Codes of Practice.
- be expected to observe the terms of the Equal Opportunities policy.

Terms and conditions
- This is a permanent post to start on 15th July and will have a trial period of six months
- The salary, paid monthly is £xx,xxx.xx per annum for a 39 hour week Monday to Friday. Hours worked in excess of 39 per week or on a Saturday will be paid at time and a half. Hours worked on a Sunday or between 11pm and 9am will be paid at double time.
- It is to be expected that some evenings and Saturdays will be worked, particularly just before and during a Production Week. Subsistence at the current union rate will be paid if the Construction Manager currently lives more than 40 miles from this theatre.
- This theatre is an Equal Opportunities Employer and employees will be expected to observe the terms of the equal opportunities policy which reads.
- This theatre is committed to the principle of Equality of Opportunity and Access.
- The policy applies without regard to gender, race, colour, ethnic or national origin, religion, disability, age, marital status, family responsibilities or sexual orientation.

description. These reviews should also take place for all existing members of staff in the form of regular 'chats' about how work is going, and a formal annual appraisal interview. It is important that appraisal is a confidential two-way process, which talks about facts, not feelings, and about performance, not personality.

As well as the manager talking about how they feel the job is going, the interviews should be an opportunity for the member of staff to clarify their role, state where they see their contribution leading, and suggest changes to their job description in order to fulfil their potential or to make the job more challenging. They should be encouraged to assess their own performance and that of their manager. At the end of the appraisal interview, new targets should have been set, standards of performance agreed, and any training needs settled.

STAGE MANAGEMENT

A good stage management team is vital to any production and any production manager. They are the department that attends rehearsals in the rehearsal room, and are responsible for relaying all information from rehearsals and the director to the rest of the organization – and just as important, conveying information from the rest of the organization back to the rehearsal room and the director. Stage management is the one department in professional theatre where the staffing level is set by rules rather than by common sense (although they often produce the same result).

All professional productions will work to one of the Equity Agreements, which stipulate how the stage management team should be made up. The team will be headed by a company manager or stage manager or company stage manager, and will consist of at

---

Stage Management Team Sizes

These are set out in the various union agreements as follows:

West End Agreement:
Musicals: At least one stage manager or company and stage manager, one DSM and one ASM (none of whom shall act or understudy).
Straight plays: At least one stage manager or company and stage manager, one DSM (neither of whom shall act or understudy) and either an ASM (who shall neither act nor understudy), or an understudy with stage management duties.

Subsidised Repertory Agreement:
One team of not less than one stage manager, one DSM and one ASM (none of whom shall act or understudy).
At least one more DSM must be employed if rehearsing or presenting a production in a second auditorium.

ITC (Small-Scale Touring) Agreement:
For a company of nine or more performers: two dedicated stage managers.
For a company of fewer than nine performers: one dedicated stage manager.
For a minimal show with fewer than four performers it may be possible to operate without a dedicated stage manager.

USA – Actors' Equity Association:
LORT Agreement (League of Regional Theatres):
One stage manager and at least one first assistant stage manager depending on the category of the theatre.

OPPOSITE: *An example of a job description.*

least one deputy stage manager (DSM) and a number of assistant stage managers (ASMs).

The stage management department is responsible for:

- the well-being of performers, especially the actors;
- attending rehearsals, and making sure the rehearsal room is satisfactory;
- communication to and from the rehearsal room and director to the rest of the organization;
- acquiring furniture and props which are not going to be made (propping);
- hiring furniture and props which are not being made or propped;
- making paperwork props (letters, documents, newspapers) and food props, and providing crockery, utensils and glassware;
- in some organizations making all the props;
- preparing nearly all the paperwork lists needed to run performances;
- preparing the stage and backstage areas for each performance;
- running the show in performance;
- returning all props at the end of the production;

How stage management are contracted will depend on the set-up of the theatre or production company. If it is a one-off production, the team will be contracted for that production only. If there is a season of shows they may be contracted for the whole season, or the team may get bigger and smaller as the workload changes. It is an advantage to have continuity in a stage management department because of maintaining local contacts and knowledge, as well as developing an understanding of resident members of staff and how they like to work.

It can work well to have a stage manager and perhaps one DSM who are on permanent contracts, to employ ASMs as required for shows or seasons of shows, and to have a second DSM where shows overlap. Building-based production managers will work out staffing schedules with their stage manager and see if they can fit the requirements within the budget.

The head of the stage management department (whatever their job title: here we will be calling them the stage manager, or SM) will be mainly office based. If they do work on the production in performance, they will keep themselves as free of duties as possible to be able to problem-solve, or to stand in for others in case of illness or injury.

The Deputy Stage Manager (DSM)

The DSM is the member of the team in closest touch with the production. He or she will attend every rehearsal both in the rehearsal room and in the theatre, and will play a vital role at every performance. They are what is known as 'on the book'. This means that they are responsible for producing the prompt copy (or book) for the production, and using it to run the show in performance. The prompt copy is the most important document in any production, as it will eventually hold all the information to enable performances to happen, especially all the cues.

In performance the DSM will sit at the prompt desk, out of view to the audience,

Blacks

All stage management and technicians should wear black clothing during performances, unless they are required to be in costume for 'in view' scene changes. It is part of the Equity contract that these will be supplied and maintained by the theatre. The blacks should extend to footwear, and arms and legs should be fully covered.

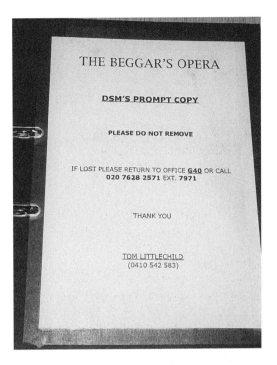

either in the wings (hence prompt corner) or in a soundproof box at the back of the auditorium. The prompt desk is the communication centre for the show. As well as headset communication (known as 'cans') between the DSM and all operators, it has a number of switches that operate cue lights. These are used in case the headset system fails, or where it would be inappropriate to use the headset, for instance for actors' entrances. There is usually a red light for 'standby' (which flashes until acknowledged by the operator) and a green one for 'go'. The prompt desk will also have paging systems to front of house and backstage.

Cues

As already described, a cue (normally written as 'Q') is an instruction to a technician or member of stage management to do something – perhaps change a lighting state, play a sound effect or move a piece of scenery. In professional theatre, no technical changes happen unless the operator is instructed to do them by the DSM. This is known as 'being cued', and each cue is always preceded by a warning, known as a 'standby'.

During rehearsals – and especially once the show moves into the theatre – the DSM writes all cues in the book. Each cue is numbered in sequence for each department, and this number corresponds to the number of the cue in the lighting board or on a technician's running plot. The DSM may also cue actors to make their entrances, particularly if they need to enter as something happens, rather than on a specific line of the script.

In the book, cues are always written in pencil so they can be changed easily, as they are frequently, in production week and afterwards.

A prompt copy on the outside.

The DSM will follow the script in the prompt copy, making backstage and front-of-house calls as written in 'the book', giving cues as written and rehearsed, and making notes of anything that goes wrong or differently in the performance.

Depending on the show, the ability to read music can be an advantage or a requirement for the DSM. They certainly need to have a musical ear and a good sense of timing. They also need to build up a rapport and feeling of mutual trust with the director. Depending on the director, the DSM may need to be their personal assistant, sounding board, whipping post, confidante or go-between. They should also be trusted by members of the cast, who will look for the DSM's support in the way they set up and run the rehearsal room, and how they help when lines are forgotten (prompting). Some actors may want the DSM's opin-

35

A prompt desk (see page 34).

ion as to what is working and what isn't in a scene or performance. The DSM must therefore judge what sort of a relationship each actor and director expects to have with them.

Production managers should be aware of the strengths and weaknesses of their DSMs and, in conjunction with the HOD, allocate the DSM to the shows and directors that will make best use of their skills. Being 'on the book' for a show in rehearsal is a full time activity, and it is therefore not practical (or affordable) to try and schedule the DSM to work on anything else during this time.

The Assistant Stage Manager (ASM)

The ASM is the most junior member of the stage management team. Under the stage manager's instruction he or she will probably be responsible for:

- acquiring props and furniture for shows in rehearsal;
- producing paperwork props and food props for rehearsals and performances;
- making or adapting props if there is not a prop-making department;
- setting up for, and running shows in performance;
- assisting the DSM in the rehearsal room and sometimes deputising for them.

Especially with building-based companies, ASMs are likely to be working on more than one show at once, and must divide their working day between setting up for and running the performance (which will usually be at night), and preparing for the next production. There may be only one ASM on a simple production, but two or more

Rehearsal Rooms

It is unusual for professional productions to rehearse on stage until a few days before the show opens, and it will be stage management's responsibility to find, set up and trouble-shoot rehearsal rooms. Some companies are lucky enough to have their own rehearsal rooms, either in the theatre building or nearby. Others have permanent or semi-permanent arrangements to be able to use places such as church halls, sports centres or other people's theatres.

(one looking after each side of the stage) for bigger shows.

In performances, unless there is a dedicated props running crew, the ASM will be responsible for setting, checking and dealing with props and furniture before and during the show. This may involve doing on-stage scene changes, handing props to actors, making any food and drink that is consumed as part of the show, and looking after the well-being of performers generally.

All stage management needs to have extremely good people skills, a sound technical knowledge, and to be able to pay attention to detail and remain calm under pressure. They will also be good at taking and passing on instructions, and individually will be extremely well organized. Stage management should

A props table marked up ready for a performance. Photo: Peter Johnson Booth

A rehearsal room. Photo: Julia Mathes

prepare their paperwork on the basis that, should they be hit by the proverbial bus, someone else would be able to set up or run the show from that paperwork.

They must also be adept at dealing with individuals' artistic temperament that may be adversely affected by the pressure of rehearsing and performing, by the frustration of limited resources, and – hopefully rarely – by an over-inflated ego. Inevitably, rehearsing and preparing any production in a limited amount of time is a stressful business. If stage management are told forcibly or rudely that a prop is wrong, a costume is uncomfortable or a cue light is being given at the wrong time, it is probably no more than an expression of an actor's or director's overall anxiety. All theatre staff, but particularly stage management, need to be able to recognize artistic temperament for what it is, and not take it personally. They should note the 'problem', do something about it if they can – and move on.

Stage management are the safety net for any production, particularly once it is in performance. If there is a problem, for example a costume that is damaged or a door that is sticking, an actor will tell stage management, and even though it is not their direct responsibility, they will be expected to sort the problem out. They will do this by talking to the department concerned, or if they are not available, by doing running repairs themselves and talking to the department later. They will also record any problems in the Show Report (*see* page 171).

In building-based organizations, stage management will have their own office, which should be close to the stage. It should be well equipped with telephones and computers, with a separate desk for each member of the team. Ideally there will also be a props and furniture store, for which stage management will have responsibility. There will also need to be space to store items acquired for a production. For one-off productions, or if the rehearsal room is out of the building, stage management will set up an office there with easy links back to the theatre or production base.

Particularly with small-scale productions or when on tour, members of stage management may be required to undertake other duties. Thus the DSM may be required to operate the lighting or sound board, the ASM may also be responsible for wardrobe, and the stage manager may be required to re-light the show in each venue. There may also be van-driving requirements, and a responsibility for putting up and taking down the set.

Career Development

Stage management are most likely to have trained at a drama school. This will have given them a background in all technical theatre departments, and practical experience in everything that goes into preparing and running theatre productions. They will also have studied theatre history, literature and historical periods, and will have had training in all the practical and paperwork aspects of the job of stage management. They should also be up-to-date with legislation, particularly where it relates to health and safety.

Stage management will get their first jobs as ASMs. As they gain experience, they may have the chance to take over the running of a show from the DSM (this is called 'book cover'), or they may be asked to be 'on the book' for a small or straightforward show to give them experience. The career route is then usually to gain experience as a DSM in a variety of theatres before becoming a stage manager.

Over time the stage manager will accumulate experience in different venues and on bigger and bigger productions. It is very common for stage managers to become production managers, and in some small organizations the jobs of SM and Production Manager are one and the same.

It is important to realize that all three stage management positions are different from each other, and call for different skills and abilities. For example, if someone is an outstanding DSM, they may not make a good stage manager, or even want to be considered for this post.

Stage management, like actors, will be contracted under one of the Equity Agreements, which set out minimum rates of pay, overtime arrangements and working conditions. As

A stage management office.

with all theatre staff who work on performances, they should expect to work every evening and most Saturdays. Stage management overtime can be expensive if they work very long hours, and from the theatre's point of view it may be more economical to employ more staff and to limit the amount of overtime worked.

Amateur Stage Management

Amateur companies tend to structure their stage management teams differently from professionals, in that the stage manager is on the book, but does not attend rehearsals. However, this can lead to major problems due to one person having too much to do in a short period of time, without enough detailed knowledge of the production. As will be explained later, stage management involvement with all rehearsals is vital, and a production manager for an amateur company would do well to encourage their SM team to follow the professional model.

STAGE TECHNICIANS

Stage technicians are likely to be employed by a theatre rather than a production company. The number in this department will depend on the size and complexity of the venue, and the type of productions it stages. Quite often there is a very small permanent staff supplemented by **casuals** for the changeover from one show to another, and for running big shows.

Casuals are employed on an hourly basis. Often they have other jobs, or are students, but have an interest in theatre and in earning some extra money. They usually work in the evenings and at weekends. It is important that a theatre has a good pool of skilled casuals: by using them regularly their skills can be built up, and they may then be considered for permanent jobs as these arise.

The head of department, if there is one,

Flying

'Flying' is the term used for suspending and moving scenery and lighting equipment above the stage. There are three main methods of flying: hemp, counterweight and power flying. **Hemp flying** involves ropes that run from the fly floor over pulleys on the grid to the flying bar. This relies on muscle power to move the flying bar. **Counterweight flying** uses steel cables to attach the flying bar to a cradle that runs up the side wall of the stage and can be loaded with weights to balance the object being flown. The flying bar is moved by pulling the cradle up or down. **Power flying** uses motors, often controlled by a computer, as individual lifting points or to move a flying bar.

may be called the technical manager or technical stage manager or, confusingly, in a presenting house, the resident stage manager (although they will not carry out Equity stage management duties). Members of the department are called the crew. Their job titles may be stage crew, stage technicians, stage daymen, stage staff, or flymen. In a smaller venue there may not be an HOD, but the staff may report directly to the production manager. In a presenting house, or a producing house that also receives tours, they will 'get in', fit up and run incoming productions, and will be instructed by touring stage management staff.

Job Description

Stage technicians are responsible for handling scenery and operating stage equipment during the fit-up and performances, for preparing and maintaining the stage and its surrounding areas, and particularly for flying. They will work mainly in the evenings but may have

STANDARD CONTRACT FOR SUBSIDISED REPERTORY AND REPERTOIRE
AND FOR THEATRE-IN-EDUCATION AND YOUNG PEOPLE'S THEATRE COMPANIES
Approved by Equity and TMA.

STAGE MANAGEMENT CONTRACT

Artist/Agent Copies: WHITE   Equity's copy: BLUE   Manager's Copy: YELLOW

THIS CONTRACT made this . . . . day of . . . . 200. . .

BETWEEN . . . . (hereinafter called "the Manager")

of . . . . of the one part

AND . . . . (hereinafter called "the Artist")

of . . . .

. . . .

. . . . (hereinafter called "the Artist's Home Address") of the other part

The name and address of the Artist's Agent may be inserted in this space. . . . .

NOTE: This Contract shall incorporate the provisions set out in Schedules 1 to 3 of the Subsidised Repertory Agreement. A copy of the Agreement shall be provided by the Manager to the Equity Deputy.

1. The Manager hereby engages the Artist to perform the duties of:

Two of these   *   (a) Stage Manager
sub-clauses must be *   (b) Deputy Stage Manager
deleted and initialled *   (c) Assistant Stage Manager
by both parties   In connection with T.I.E. (Delete if not applicable)

At ....

or in such other theatres and towns as the Manager may require

Period of Engagement   **2.** (A) The engagement shall commence on the ....
day of .... 200 ...., and shall subsist

One of these   *   (a) For an indefinite period terminable by either party giving .... days
sub-clauses must be   (not being less than 28 days, or 56 days in the case of TIE) notice in writing, such notice not to expire
deleted and initialled   before the last performance of a production in which the Artist is rehearsing or appearing at the date
by both parties   on which such notice is given.

        *   (b) For a guaranteed period until .... day of .... 200..............

Salary   **3.** The Manager shall pay to the Artist the sum of £ .... per week (exclusive of subsistence) for a maximum of eight performances per week (Monday to Saturday), but not more than two on anyone day (unless the Artist is engaged in connection with TIE/YPT, when the provisions of Clause 3 of Appendix 3 may apply).

Subsistence Allowance 4.   A Subsistence Allowance of £ .... per week or part thereof for the first 13 weeks of the engagement where the Artist's address is 25 miles or more from the rehearsal/performance venue (see 1.10.1., also 1.11.4. for weekly Travel Allowance).

Touring Allowance   **5.** (a) Touring Allowance of £ .... per day or £ ...., per week or part thereof when on tour (see 1.10.2.).
Delete if
inapplicable   (b) The Manager requires the Artist, in receipt of touring allowance, to reside within 15 miles of the theatre in which he/she is performing (20 miles in the case of a theatre in the Greater London area) (see 1.13.5.2.)

Transport   **6.** The Manager shall give the Artist the appropriate standard class rail fare Including available reduced price tickets) from the Artist's address to the place where he/she is required to rehearse or perform at the beginning of the engagement and back at the end of the engagement.

Personal Pension   ***7.** The Manager shall pay separately to the Artist £ ....of the gross weekly salary for the Artist to pay into
Scheme   his/her Personal Pension Scheme.
Delete if
inapplicable

As Witness the hands of the parties on the day, month and year first above written.

.... Manager   ....Artist

Manager's Tax Ref. No.	Artist's N,I. No.	Artist's Equity No.	Artist's V.A.T. No.	Artist's Sch. D. No.

Artist's name for National Insurance purposes if different from stage name...

An Equity stage management contract.

A hemp fly floor.

If there is a technical manager, he or she will attend production meetings and may have to cost for additional equipment needed for the production. They will work with the production manager in scheduling the crew requirements of the fit-up, and be responsible for the show crew in performances. During the planning stages, they will work with the designer and lighting designer on the masking of the show.

As well as having excellent technical skills and experience, technical managers will have a good knowledge of health and safety, particularly as it applies to flying. A working knowledge of computerized drawing packages is also an advantage.

Stage technicians will be skilled in using stage machinery and particularly in counterweight flying, in moving large pieces of scenery and in rigging scenery, in masking and in stage equipment. Really good technicians are also sensitive to the requirements of a production, and can time scenery movements to fit exactly with pieces of music, carry out scene changes in complete silence, and keep out of the way when artistic temperament is prevalent.

Career Development

Permanently employed stage technicians may have started working on stage while still at school. They may have decided on some training where they will have developed skills and had experience of the work of other departments, or they may have started as a casual and worked their way up. Stage technicians can progress to become technical managers in large venues, or they may move into stage or production management. Increasingly they may decide to improve their skills and become much sought-after riggers or operators of computer control systems.

Wherever they work, they should appreciate that they are in a potentially dangerous

daytime duties, which could include helping out in the scenic workshop, building maintenance, driving, or looking after the store if the theatre has one. They may also 'multi-skill' and work as members of the electrics department, particularly as followspot operators or stage electricians.

A counterweight fly floor.

environment and, as with all staff, take care that their work does not endanger their own safety or that of others.

Stage technicians will work mainly in the theatre itself, and are likely to have an office or crew room as their base. They will need the usual office requirements, changing facilities and storage for equipment and tools. They may work in the theatre's stores and work-shops, take pieces of the set to the rehearsal room, and perhaps attend a final run-through of a show in rehearsal. Occasionally they may go out on tour with one of the theatre's pro-ductions or be used to help at the fit-up and strike of a tour or a transfer.

Getting involved as a member of the stage crew for an amateur company is an excellent way of starting to get experience in backstage theatre work. Professional theatres often recruit from local amateur companies when they need to add to their list of casuals.

Working out masking from a side elevation.

SCENIC CONSTRUCTION

The construction department is responsible for the building and delivery onto stage of all items of scenery within agreed budgets and schedules. The department will only exist in a producing theatre, as production companies will use scenery contractors to do this work. Amateur companies may have members of the company who build scenery, but particularly on large-scale shows and musicals, are more likely to hire their scenery.

Until fairly recently, the head of the workshop was known as the master carpenter. This phrase is no longer used because it is gender specific and does not reflect the wide range of materials that a construction department is expected to use.

Today the HOD may be called the construction manager, the head of workshop, or the scenic workshop supervisor; we will call him or her the **construction manager**. Depending upon the set-up of the organization, they will have a number of staff responsible to them. There is likely to be a deputy, plus a number of craftsmen who may work in just timber (carpenters), just steel (metalworkers), or more usefully in either material (workshop technicians). In a large set-up there may also be a draftsman and an administrator, and other support staff.

The Scenic Workshop

It is not essential for the scenic workshop to be in the main theatre building, but there are advantages if it is. It will not be necessary to

Making scenery. Photo: *The Leader*

A timber set.

transport the finished set to the theatre, and the production manager, along with the designer and other members of the creative team, will not have to make special trips to see the set being built. Construction staff will be much more integrated into the whole organization, and it will be much easier for them to attend meetings, talk to production and administrative staff, and use facilities such as catering.

The equipment likely to be found in a scenic workshop includes the following:

- crosscut saw (for cutting lengths of timber);
- table saw and/or panel saw (for cutting sheets of timber);
- morticer and tenoner (for making timber joints);
- pillar drill;
- metal-cutting machine (cold-cut, not abrasive wheel);

- welding machines (mig or tig, not arc);
- angle grinders (for cleaning up welds);
- compressed air tools (staplers, nailers, wrenches);
- bandsaw;
- battery-operated screwdrivers (often called Makitas after one of the manufacturers). These are essential to almost every technical theatre department;
- hand tools such as hammers, chisels and planes.

The scenic workshop space is sometimes shared with the scene painters, and this calls for liaison and understanding between the HODs and staff to ensure that the work of both departments can be carried out successfully.

The Construction Manager's Role

The Construction Manager will attend production meetings, and will work from the model,

A crosscut saw.

A table saw.

groundplan and working drawings supplied by the set designer. They will also arrange a separate meeting with the designer to discuss the set in detail. They will cost the construction of the set in terms of materials and time, and will consider how to use the available workshop space. Other members of the department may well become involved at this stage, as this is when decisions will be made about how to build the show.

There will also be discussions with other departments who have an interest in the set:

- scene painters who have to paint the finished set, and may need it in a specific order;
- the technical manager who may have to fly items of the set;
- props who may be required to carve pieces of the set, or produce other embellishments;
- the electrics department who may need to add practical lights;
- the sound department, particularly to do with the siting of speakers.

Safety in the Workshop

With such a large number of machines and activities, the workshop can be a particularly dangerous place.

Particular attention needs to be paid to matters concerning risk assessment and maintenance. There will need to be codes of practice for the safe use of each piece of equipment.

Staff need to be aware of the dangers of multiple activities taking place. Noise is also likely to be an issue. This is covered further in Chapter 5.

The construction manager will then discuss with the production manager how they intend to build the show and anything to do with fitting it up, particularly how long this will take,

A panel saw: this is safer to use for cutting sheet material than a table saw.

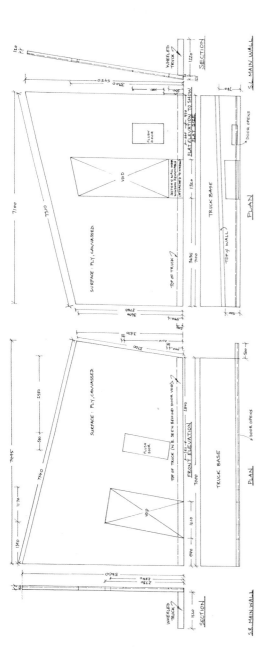

The working drawing of the piece of scenery shown on page 45. Designer: Charles Edwards

ABOVE: A bandsaw with its safety instructions.

or running it. A good construction manager will also have ideas about what could be used from stock, how the set could be built to make touring it easier, and what might be useful stock at the end of a run.

It is important that the production manager has a good relationship with the head of construction, as they rely on them to produce a well built, fully working set, safely, on time and within budget. They will work particularly closely during the fit-up. The construction manager will also be aware of any shortcomings in the design, and should talk to the production manager about these before they become a problem.

As well as skills in carpentry, metalwork, budgeting and man management, the construction manager will need to have some knowledge of structural engineering (for scenery which supports weight), physics (how will scenery behave under given conditions), mechanics (how will the scenery move), and a good knowledge of and commitment to health and safety.

Workshop Staff

Workshop staff may have had specialist training in carpentry and metalwork, or they may have attended a specialist theatre crafts

Handling scenery during a fit-up.
Photo: Laurence Burns

Additional Staff

In addition to full-time staff, the production manager or the construction manager should have a list of:
- skilled casuals who can be used to supplement workshop staff
- unskilled casuals to carry out straightforward tasks (cutting lots of timber, degreasing steel, unloading lorries)
- experienced casuals for the fit-up and strike
- freelance staff and construction companies who can be used if there is too much scenery for it all to be built in-house

course. Alternatively they may have more general experience, perhaps in the building industry, and have decided to try their hand in a theatre environment; or they may have worked their way up from being a stage casual. During their career they may progress through a theatre workshop or scenery construction company before, perhaps, starting a company of their own.

Scenic construction staff will mainly work a standard week of up to forty hours. They may be required to work overtime if there is a particularly big set to be built (though this would have to be allowed for in the costing) and, as with all departments, they should expect unusual hours of work during the production week.

They will work particularly long hours during the changeover from one show to another. This may involve striking the set of the previous show on a Saturday night after the final performance and fitting up the next show on the Sunday, after only the minimum allowed break and this is a time of very physical work.

Starting to paint a cloth.

SCENE PAINTING

Texturing a piece of scenery.

This is a highly specialized department involving a number of very individual skills. The staff are responsible for all paint and texture finishes on the scenery.

Once again, staffing levels will vary enormously. A building-based theatre company may have a head scenic artist and a number of more junior staff, or it may decide to use freelance scenic artists as and when it needs them; this can be a sensible option if the amount of painting work varies throughout the year. There are a large number of freelance painters and companies who specialize in scene-painting, and it may be that a designer will want a particular painter to be responsible for their show.

Scenic artists may have had a fine art training, or they may have been on a specialist theatre crafts or design course. They will be used to working with a wide variety of materials and techniques to produce the required finished look. They will start their career in a

The finished cloth on stage. Photo: Mike Rothwell

junior position or as an assistant, and may work their way up to a head scenic artist, or decide fairly early on to work in a freelance capacity. Depending on their training, scene-painting is quite often the starting-off point on the route to becoming a designer.

The painters' major reference is the scale model, but they will want to have initial discussions with the set designer before providing a costing for the show or starting work on the actual scenery. They will produce samples of paint or texture finishes and ask the designer to choose which they want. Production managers need to allow time for this sampling process during the costing of a design as one technique may be much more expensive than another. Painters will also want to see the designer frequently during the painting of the show to make sure that they are producing the right 'look'.

As with other HODs, the head scenic artist will attend production meetings and produce time and materials estimates for painting the show. A particular consideration for scenic

A scenic artist working from a piece of the model. Photo: GSMD archives

51

The Paintframe

A paintframe is an important piece of equipment in a paintshop. It is a large, vertical wooden frame onto which backcloths can be stretched, or built scenery can be fixed. A mechanism then enables the artists to reach any part of the cloth or scenery without having to go up and down ladders. Either the whole frame moves up and down and the painters stay on the floor, or the painters get onto a gantry or bridge, which then moves them (and their paints and brushes and other equipment) up and down.

artists is the need to use a paintframe. If the theatre has one, scheduling its use is very important. If it does not, a very large, clear floor area will be needed to paint cloths, or it may be necessary to hire paintframe time in another theatre or specialist workshop.

The scenic artist will liaise with the production manager and construction manager about the order in which the built scenery will arrive in the paintshop. He or she will want to have the pieces that need the most work first, and the simpler pieces last. If there is a lot of texturing on pieces of scenery, it will need to be decided whether the construction or props departments are going to be involved, or whether it is entirely the responsibility of the scenic artists.

As with construction staff, scenic artists will usually work a basic week during the preparation of a show, but they may need to put in some overtime towards the end to make sure the set is ready to go on stage. Additionally there may be the question of painting the stage floor for a show, though this is often done overnight. There may also be late

A paint bridge in its lowest position.

A paint bridge in a raised position.

night work to complete notes from the designer once the set is seen on stage under light, or to complete jobs that could not be done before the set was assembled. The timing of this work is discussed in Chapter 7.

PROP-MAKING

This is another very specialized department, and one that may not exist in all building-based companies. **Prop-makers** are responsible for making or adapting props and furniture as required by the designer. A prop (abbreviation for 'property') is any object handled by the cast but the prop-making department can also be expected to produce set dressing (objects used to give a period feel to the set) and soft furnishings (curtains and cushions). They may work with the wardrobe department if there are constructional or fantasy costumes, and with electrics if there are props that need to light up or work in some other way. There may also be items of the set that the props department will work on, particularly if carving is involved.

Prop-makers need a huge range of skills, artistic flare, and also experience in using a wide range of very specialized and unusual materials. They need to be expert problem solvers. They will work from the model, and from drawings and reference material supplied by the designer, but they may also want to have discussions with the director, the designer and stage management about how a prop will be used by the actors. They may want to call actors to their workshop to try out prototypes, or to work with the actor to decide exactly how a prop needs to function.

Training for prop-makers is likely to be on specialist theatre craft or design courses, and, as with scenic artists, they may be budding designers. They can start as an assistant and work their way up with the possibility of becoming freelance, or working for a specialist company.

A prop-making department is a huge asset to a theatre. Not only does it add to what can

ABOVE: **Making fake bricks for a set.**
Photo: *The Leader*

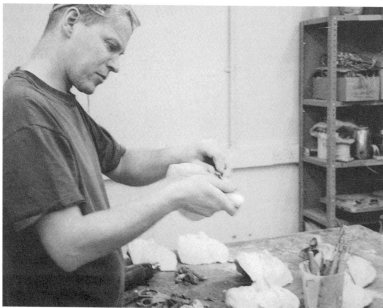

OPPOSITE:
A designer's drawing for making a piece of furniture.

LEFT: **Carving a prop.**

be produced for a show, but over time it will increase the amount of stock props and furniture available for future productions.

If there are no prop-making staff, all the responsibility for props and furniture will fall to stage management working in conjunction with the designer. Much of this will then have to be hired, which is 'dead money'.

Props will need their own workshop space with specialist equipment to enable a wide range of tasks to be carried out. They will need most of the timber and metalworking equipment found in a scenic workshop, equipment and space for working with fabrics, as well as carving and modelling tools.

It may be that props can share some of the equipment in the scenic workshop, but this will need careful scheduling and liaison. It is generally better if each department has its own equipment, partly because they will each

then be responsible for the maintenance and safe usage of all the tools in their area.

The hours of work for prop staff will be very similar to those of the scenic construction and scene-painting departments. During fit-ups and production week they will be expected to install their work on stage, and to attend technical and dress rehearsals to make sure that performers and technicians know how it works, and that it is functioning correctly. They may then have to work overtime, once it has been seen and used on stage, to make minor adjustments.

The list of items a props department might produce includes:

• furniture: making from scratch, or adapting or restoring an existing piece;
• soft furnishings: making curtains, and installing the mechanism to operate them;

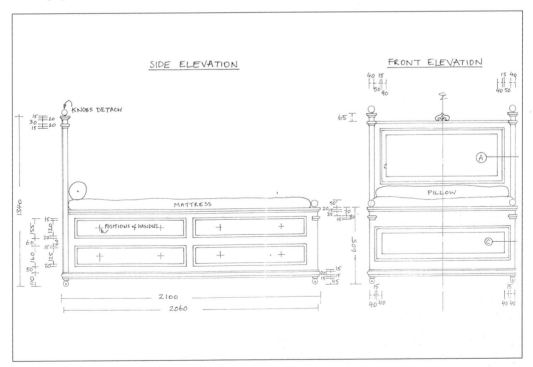

A designer's drawing for making a piece of furniture. Designer: Charles Edwards.

Using props equipment safely. Photo: Laurence Burns

OPPOSITE: **A lighting board set up in the auditorium.** Photo: The Leader

- sculpting items, either as part of the set or as sculptures in their own right;
- making or adapting objects to do unusual things: flowers that grow or wilt on cue, weapons that produce blood, or props that appear to break every night;
- creatures;
- tricks.

Each prop-maker and each department will have their own skills and preferred areas of work, and a production manager will appreciate this, and will concentrate on these strengths whenever possible. Some larger organizations will have separate props-buying departments who will work closely with the designer and buy or hire props for a production, where this is more economical than making them.

Electrics

In most building-based organizations this department is likely to have a permanent staff because they have a responsibility not only for productions, but also for the electrical mainte-

nance of the building. The electrics department is responsible for rigging the lighting for the production, using information from the lighting plan provided by the lighting designer. They use specialist equipment, and the design will usually be based on the theatre's stock, with additional equipment hired in as needed. They may also use computer programs to produce information about the lighting rig, such as how much equipment needs to be hired, the weight of each lighting bar, the amount of gel needed to colour the lights, and the circuit that will power each lantern.

There is a large range of theatre lighting equipment available. This can vary in power from a few watts to ten kilowatts, and in size from 50mm to more than a metre across. It can also vary in complexity, from a lantern that floods light everywhere, to an 'intelligent light source' that can be made to move and change the colour and shape of the beam of light under the control of the lighting board. Lanterns are powered by dimmers controlled by the lighting board, which is almost always computerized. As well as the brightness of

each lantern, the board controls how quickly each lighting state fades or builds, and can run through a series of states one after another. A modern board will also control colour changers, smoke machines and fans as well as auditorium and backstage working lights. Much of the skill of an electrics department is knowing what equipment can do, and how to use and maintain it.

Once the lighting and the set are in place, a member of the electrics department will go to each lantern in the rig and focus each unit under instruction from the lighting designer. They may be able to reach some of the equipment from catwalks (known as bridges), but, particularly for equipment rigged over the stage, specialist access equipment will also need to be used. There are two main types of specialist access used in the theatre: a tallescope – an extendable vertical metal ladder on wheels; and a genie – a working platform on the top of an electrically powered extendable mast. Both devices are potentially dangerous to use, and codes of practice should be followed closely (*see* Appendix 1 for examples).

A tallescope.

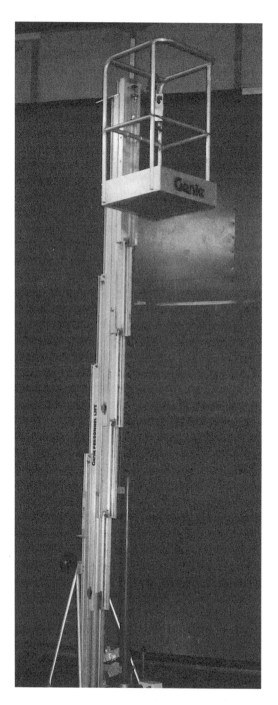

A genie hoist.

Once all the lighting has been rigged, focused and coloured, the department will work with the lighting designer in plotting the lighting for each scene (*see* Chapter 8). It involves a member of the electrics department operating the lighting board and recording the brightness of each lantern in each lighting state.

Electrics are also responsible for producing any working electrical items. These are known as practicals, and can vary from domestic light fittings to special effects such as explosions, and from working household appliances to pieces of the set that light up. They are also responsible for any projection, for additional equipment such as smoke machines or wind machines, and for running in the power for any stage machinery such as motors or winches. Offstage they will set up 'working light' so that actors, stage management and technicians can see to do their jobs in the reduced light levels backstage, and they may also be responsible for the electrical maintenance and safety of the whole building.

The electrics staff, their equipment and their area of the building are all known as LX; the head of department is the **chief LX**. Depending on the set-up of the organization, they will have a deputy and a number of assistants. The department will also call on casuals to help with rigging and focusing, and perhaps to operate followspots, or be responsible for LX duties on stage during a performance. As well as preparing for a production during the rehearsal period, most members of the LX department will work on the shows in performance at night.

The route into an electrics department is often from being a casual, but there are also specialist and generalized theatre courses that can be the start of a career in LX. Electricians usually start off as assistants and then work their way up through the department as they gain experience. As described in Chapter 2, it is sometimes the role of an in-house chief LX to design the lighting for productions. This can be the start on the ladder to becoming a freelance lighting designer. It is also quite common for a chief LX to become a production manager.

The chief LX will attend production meetings and produce a costing for the production – even though, unlike other departments, their major source of information, the lighting plan, will not be available at this stage. This is because the lighting designer will not be able to produce their plan until the show has been rehearsed and it is known where the performers will be standing, and therefore where the equipment needs to be in order to light them. The costing will be based on any special requirements that the lighting designer knows are going to be needed, the design of any practicals, plus global figures for gel and consumables.

Although LX staff are answerable to the production manager, and take most of their instruction from the lighting designer, they will also need to liaise with:

- the set designer over the look of any practicals;
- the scenery department over any LX requirements in the set;
- the props department about any LX requirements in a prop;
- stage management about backstage requirements.

All LX operators will be cued by the DSM during on-stage rehearsals and performances.

The electrics department is likely to have an office and a workshop in the theatre building, and will also spend much of their working time in the control room where the lighting board is situated.

In an amateur company there may be some individuals with electrics experience that they

---

The Chief LX and Production Manager

As a production manager, a good relationship and mutual trust between you and the chief LX are very important. They are responsible for a sizeable part of the production work, especially once the show moves into the theatre. They have to co-ordinate a number of tasks, which, if not ready for the appropriate time in production week, can cause major delays and expense.

---

may have gained through casual work at a professional theatre. The production manager will need to ensure that they understand the dangers of working with electricity and at height, and perhaps encourage them to undertake training in these areas.

SOUND

Sound is becoming a more and more specialized area of work in the theatre. Once dealt with by the electrics department and before that by stage management, it now has technology that requires people with specific skills and knowledge to be employed. A sound designer is now engaged for nearly every show, and the sound department is responsible for rigging all equipment for a production and operating it to the designer's instruction.

The source of sound will come from recordings prepared by the sound designer or from microphones on stage, worn by the actors or amongst the band. The sound is controlled by a mixing desk before being sent via amplifiers to speakers placed around the stage and auditorium. It can also be altered by a sophisticated array of equipment such as graphic equalizers, compressors, reverberation units, noise gates and digital delay units. Depending on the set-up

A direct to disc recorder and CD player in a sound rack.

OPPOSITE: *A sound operator in performance.*

of the theatre, some or all of this equipment may need to be hired from specialist companies.

A computer can be used to control playback machines, and to select which sound goes to which speaker and at what volume. This takes a long time to set up and particularly to alter, and the production manager needs to liaise with the sound department to make sure there is enough time in production week to accommodate this technology.

Sound are also responsible for communication (known as comms) in and around the theatre. This includes cue lights, headsets (either wired or radio), video cameras and monitors, and foldback speakers (so that people in the wings can see and hear what is happening on stage). All of this needs rigging for each production. Additionally there will be permanently installed communications equipment to maintain – tannoy backstage and front of house, show relay and perhaps video relay.

The size of the sound department depends on the size of the theatre or organization

and the type of shows they perform. It may be a branch of the electrics department, or a department in its own right with an HOD, deputy and several assistants. Depending on the skills available, a freelance sound operator

History of Playback Equipment

- Wax cylinders
- 78 rpm records
- Vinyl records
- Reel-to-reel tape recorders
- Cassette players
- CDs (the first digital recordings)
- DAT (digital audio tape)
- Mini discs
- Recordable CDs (CD-Rs)
- Samplers
- Hard disc recorders
- DVD (Digital versatile disc)

Sound in Opera

In opera there is no sound reinforcement of either the singers' voices or the orchestra. Sound may be used to a limited extent for effects such as storms or battles, but these are often part of the orchestration. The sound department may be asked to relay the orchestra into the wings for off-stage singing: this would also need a video feed of the conductor, which the DSM will need as well.

is often employed on big musicals, as it can take years of practice to develop the skills to carry out live mixing on a big musical.

Members of the sound department will have developed their initial interest in theatre and sound, perhaps attended a general or sound-specific training course, and joined a sound department as a junior member. As in other areas, they can work their way up in the theatre structure, or decide to become freelance, or join a specialist sound company. They will need electronics knowledge, a knowledge of the principles of sound – and extremely sensitive ears.

WARDROBE

The wardrobe (or costume) department is responsible for providing everything worn by the performers during a production. As well as making, adapting, buying or hiring clothing, shoes and accessories, they are responsible for washing and maintaining costumes between performances, setting them in the right place before the start of the show (usually in the dressing room, but sometimes in the wings, or even on the set), and helping the actors get into and out of them, particularly if there are quick costume changes.

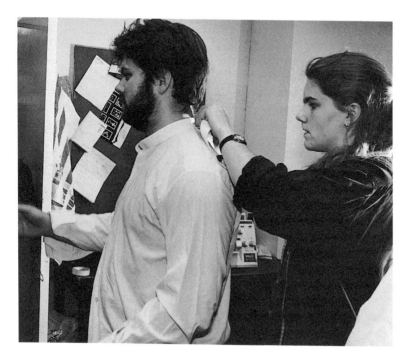

Getting an actor into costume.

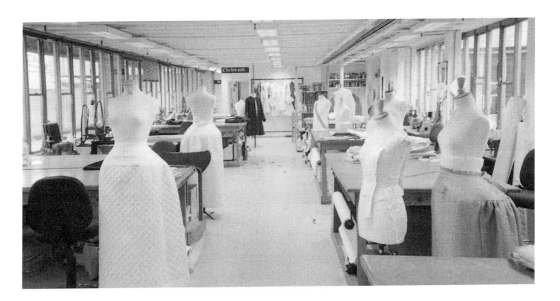

A large wardrobe workroom.

Depending on the scale of the production, this may be the work of one person or several departments. Repertory theatres may have a department headed by the wardrobe supervisor, with a cutter and a number of assistants to make the costumes, one person to carry out maintenance, and casuals to act as dressers where needed. The biggest organizations will have separate departments: a production wardrobe to make the costumes (possibly split into women's and tailoring); a running wardrobe to look after the shows in performance; and specialist departments such as wigs, millinery, costume props and dyeing. They may also have staff dedicated to the running of the wardrobe store, and they may possibly operate a hire business for other companies to use.

It is worth remembering that while you can perform a show without any scenery or sound, and with minimal lighting, you are always going to need costumes to say something about the characters, even if it is the actors wearing their own clothes.

A wardrobe department will need:

• sewing machines – industrial and domestic;
• over-lockers;
• professional steam irons;
• large cutting tables;
• washing and drying machines;
• facilities for dyeing fabric;
• a separate fitting room;
• an area to store finished costumes;
• office space for the HOD.

The nature of its work can mean that the wardrobe department is not fully understood by a production manager who may have come from a technical background. The department is then left to its own devices which, while the staff may appreciate this freedom, may also mean that things can happen without the production manager's knowledge, leading to budgetary or scheduling problems of which they may be unaware until it is too late. As with all areas, if the production manager is involved in active discussions concerning the work and potential problems, they can facilitate the work of the department and make the staff's life easier.

Fittings

Early on in the rehearsal period, the actors will need to be measured by the wardrobe department.

If costumes are being made, the actors will have to attend a number of fittings during the making process. If costumes are being bought or hired, the actor needs to be present at the shop or hire house.

This means the actors need to be released from the rehearsal room at a time when the costume designer and wardrobe staff or specialist makers are available, and if necessary, when shops are open.

This needs arranging in conjunction with their calls for rehearsal.

Wardrobe are actually little different to any other department in that they have to produce items to a director and designer's satisfaction within a financial and time budget. To do this they need specialist staff and equipment. The major differences are that their work is very labour intensive, will vary hugely from one show to the next depending on cast size and period, and the fact that the department cannot do its work without access to the actors.

The designer will supply the department with a full list of costume requirements and drawings, or other references of how they want the costumes to look. The supervisor, in conjunction with the cutter(s), will cost the designs in terms of fabric, trimmings and making time. They will also have to budget for accessories, shoes, hats, socks, tights and so on. Cutters will use their experience of period and of working with fabrics to interpret the designs into wearable costumes.

Hiring Costumes

It is possible to hire costumes for nearly all productions, and in an amateur company this may be the only way, with wardrobe staff taking on an organizational role. For a professional theatre, however, this is 'dead money', and the designer is unlikely to get exactly what they want. If resources permit, it is better to leave this option for smaller parts or chorus, and have costumes made for the major roles. These will then belong to the theatre, which means that a stock is built up, and can be used or adapted for future productions. Of course, if doing a modern piece, it makes little sense to hire the costumes, as the cost of this is likely to be the same as buying them from a high street store.

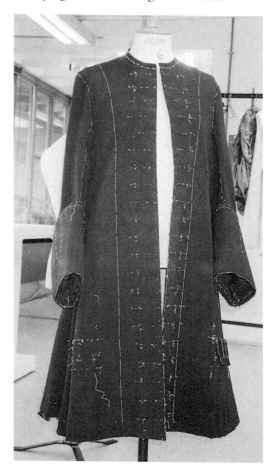

A costume being made.

Fabric samples.

Most wardrobe staff will have had specialist training on either theatre or fashion courses, and will have started work as wardrobe assistants. This can involve sewing and finishing costumes cut by the cutter, or being an assistant to the supervisor. Cutting is a particularly specialized craft, and it needs years of experience to be able to cut costumes of any period, fit them to an actor, and then pass them on to a number of assistants for completion. After training, cutters usually start as wardrobe assistants, then become an assistant cutter, and finally head cutter.

Supervisors can have worked their way through the system, although it is not absolutely necessary for them to have making skills, as theirs is an organizational role. However, they ought to have a detailed knowledge of period clothing and fabrics, and know a wide range of shops, suppliers and freelance costume makers.

After some building-based experience, many wardrobe staff decide to become freelance, as there is a big demand for makers for film, TV and non building-based stage productions.

Wardrobe staff, and particularly the supervisor, must have a very close and successful relationship with the costume designer. Even if they are designing the set as well, it is with the wardrobe department that the designer will spend most of their time.

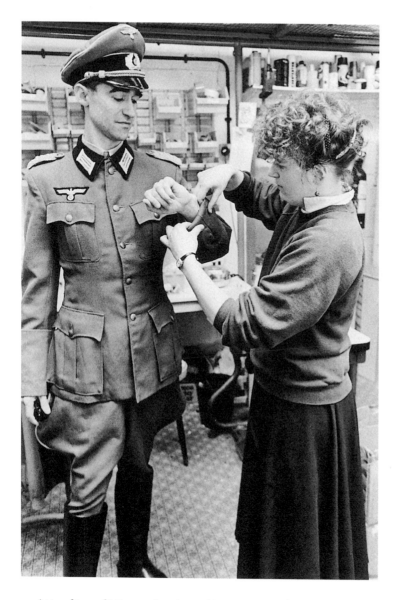

Checking the length of a cuff at a costume fitting.

Attending fittings, having discussions about how each costume is to be made and decorated, shopping for fabrics, trimmings, clothes and shoes, is a very time-consuming business, and particularly in the days before the technical rehearsal, wardrobe can expect to work long hours. Once technical and dress rehearsals start, hours are bound to be erratic as staff can only work on the costumes when the actors are not wearing them.

4 THE PRE-PRODUCTION PROCESS

OUTLINE BUDGETING

As we saw in Chapter 2, much of the running of a theatre is finance-driven. In producing theatres, for funding reasons, outline budgets may have to be published several years in advance when there can be no knowledge of what the actual productions will be. These budgets can be little more than educated guesses based on previous shows or seasons, and the type of production that might be envisaged.

What the actual show, or season of shows, is to be may be decided up to a year – and in the case of opera, several years – before the first night. The choice of production will be made by the artistic director working closely with the chief executive, and using the organization's outline budget figures.

The chief executive or senior management team can then get to work on producing a realistic budget based on what is known about the show. Different managers will use different factors to determine their budget or income targets; in the case of a producing theatre these would be as follows:

- box office income
- other income such as catering and programme sales
- acting company salaries
- the creative team fees
- marketing costs
- staging expenses

Box Office Income
This would be affected by the following:
- Is there a 'star' name? (see below)
- Is the author well known or particularly popular at the moment?
- Is there a specific target audience?
- Is the play a 'set text' in schools?
- Has the organization done a similar piece, or a piece by the same author before?
- Are there specific local links?

Star Names

- Probably a TV star but can also be a popular local amateur.
- May attract a bigger salary.
- May not want to commit at this stage, which leads to budgeting problems.
- If they will commit, they may be very useful in advanced publicity.

Other Income
Other sources of income to consider include the following:

- Is this a co-production that shares resources with another theatre or production company and tours to other venues? If so, what is the financial deal?

The table below is a matrix summarising the involvement of each person/team across each stage of the pre-production process.

Teams and roles (rows):

- Board of Directors
- Chief Executive
- Senior Management Team

The Creative Team
- Director
- Set Designer
- Costume Designer
- Lighting Designer
- Sound Designer
- Musical Director/Conductor
- Choreographer
- Fight Director

The Production Manager's Team
- Production Manager
- Stage Manager
- Deputy Stage Manager (DSM)
- Assistant Stage Manager (ASM)
- Technical Manager
- Stage Technicians
- Chief LX
- Lighting Board Operator
- Sound Operator
- Construction Manager
- Workshop Staff
- Head Scenic Artist
- Scene Painting Staff
- Head of Props
- Props Staff
- Wardrobe Supervisor
- Cutter
- Wardrobe Assistants
- Dresser

(Plus all technical staff introduced on tour of the building)

- The Acting Company
- The Band

Stages of the process (columns):

1. Decision to do the show
2. Appointment of Creative Team
3. Briefing of Creative Team
4. Design Meetings
5. White Card Model
6. Pre Production Meeting
7. Costing
8. Casting
9. Production Meeting
10. Meet and Greet
11. First Rehearsal/Model Showing/Read Thru
12. Rehearsals
13. Band call
14. Build/paint Scenery Props & Furniture
15. Acquiring Props and Furniture
16. Making/Acquiring Costumes
17. Costume fittings
18. Preparing LX design
19. Preparing sound
20. Progress Meetings
21. Final run through
22. Rigging LX
23. Fit up
24. Focus
25. Lighting
26. Technical Rehearsal
27. Dress Rehearsal
28. First Performance
29. Subsequent performances
30. Get out and returns

Legend:

- ✓ (grey/shaded) indicates full involvement
- ✓ indicates limited or non essential involvement

A summary of who is involved, and when, in making shows happen.

- Sponsorship: is the piece particularly suited to a possible sponsor?
- Programme sales: are there figures available from previous similar productions?
- Merchandising: are there specific opportunities presented by the piece?
- Catering: is there an interval, and what type and size of audience is expected?

Expenditure:
Acting Company Salaries
Answers to the following will be needed when working out a budget for a production:

- How many are there in the cast?
- For how many weeks will they be employed?
- Is there a company salary, or is each performer negotiating a separate rate?
- Is there a requirement for musicians?
- Is there any 'through' casting? (see below)

Professional actors' unions have negotiated minimum terms and conditions that theatres and production companies have to pay. As well as a minimum weekly salary, there is often a holiday entitlement of half a day per week of employment (though this is usually taken as paid time after the end of the contract), and a subsistence payment. These three are added together to give the cost to the theatre of employing each actor for a week.

Actors can be contracted to perform one show at night while they are rehearsing the next during the day. This is called 'through casting', and has the advantage that the theatre is not paying an additional actor to rehearse, and thus saves money. The disadvantages are that, unless you are prepared to pay overtime, the times when you can call the actor to rehearse are limited. The director will also have to consider whether the actor is suitable for both parts.

Expenditure: The Creative Team
A considerable cost to the theatre is that of the creative team, and the following factors would have to be considered:

- Is the director a permanent member of staff (artistic or associate director), or a guest?
- Is there one designer for set and costumes?
- Are there specific designers in mind, and what level of fees are they likely to require?
- Are any of the designers in-house staff?
- Are there any specialist requirements – for instance, musical director, fight director, choreographer, accent coach?
- What payments will have to be made to the author? For existing plays a writer, or their estate if they have been dead for less than seventy years, will receive a percentage of the box office income. If a new play is commissioned, the writer will receive a phased fee, with payments made on signing contract, on first delivery of the play, and on acceptance of the play. They will also get a fee if the play has a future life with the same management. Some theatres employ a writer-in-residence, and there may be additional grants available for this and for commissioning new writing.

Marketing Expenditure
The marketing department will usually have a standard expenditure figure for each production, although there may be savings on their costs if it is a co-production. On the other hand, additional resources may be required if it is perceived to be a difficult show to sell.

Miscellaneous Expenditure
These questions might need to be considered:

- Will there be audition expenses?
- What travel expenses will be paid to the creative team?
- Is there a need for specific research (overseas travel)?
- Are there specific hospitality requirements (sponsors or other co-producers)?

Staging Expenses

This is the area dealt with by the production manager, who will be concerned with three main budget areas: the production budget, the overtime budget, and the freelance and casuals budget. In a producing house there may be an annual budget for these areas, which the production manager divides up throughout the year. They need to decide whether the breakdown in the outline budget is correct for each production, and to adjust it accordingly.

An amateur company will need to budget for the following costs:

- materials, if they are building their own set;
- hire charges and transport costs if they are renting scenery, costumes or props;
- the hire of the theatre, unless they are lucky enough to have their own;
- charges for the services of resident professional theatre staff.

Need for Overtime

The balance between days when a theatre is closed and not earning money, and overtime costs, is a delicate one, and needs agreeing early in the planning stages.

It is almost impossible to mount a production without incurring some overtime. It can in fact be more cost effective to pay overtime so that the production can open as soon as possible and start earning income for the theatre or company.

Because of low basic wages paid in the theatre industry, many staff see overtime as a way of boosting their income to a reasonable level. This is becoming more of a problem as legislation aimed at reducing working hours is introduced.

Whether amateur or professional, if the production manager finds that, because of the nature of the shows chosen or because of how they go together to make up the season, they do not have enough budget, *they should not keep this to themselves*. It must be discussed at the earliest possible opportunity with the chief executive and artistic director before too many decisions are made. In the case of an amateur company, this will probably be with the chairman and treasurer.

The production manager may have to argue the case for more resources, and should call on figures from previous productions or seasons to support their argument. It is *the production manager's* job to be realistic about what can be achieved with the resources available, and to point this out to the managers, particularly the artistic director, who, quite rightly, will have high expectations of each and every production. 'Resources' does not just mean money: it also means the availability of suitably skilled staff, the space for them to work in, or to store work, and the amount of time there is to do any work.

The theatre or producing company then has to take these concerns on board, and either find more resources, or be prepared to limit the ambition of creative teams. Every show ever staged would have liked to have had a bigger budget, but production managers must not put themselves in the position where they try to make a show happen with unrealistic resources.

If there are to be reduced resources for one or more productions, it is only fair that the creative team are aware of this, and whoever approaches them about the project should make this clear at an early stage. It is a very poor start to a production manager's relationship with a creative team to have to be negative at their first meeting about what resources are available for their production.

READING THE SCRIPT

As soon as a show is chosen the production manager should find time to read it. This is vital in order for them to be informed about the likely requirements of the piece as they start talking to creative teams and staff about it. If it is a musical or opera, the production manager should get hold of a recording if possible, and listen to this as well as reading the script or libretto.

On the first time of reading it is best that they read the piece straight through without making too many notes, to get a sense of the piece as a whole. They should then read it through again and make notes of the following requirements, which may be written as stage directions, or be in the text itself:

- the period(s) in which the piece is set;
- the number of characters;
- the status [wealth] of the characters;
- the number of scenes and their descriptions, and the essential requirements for each scene;
- how the play moves from one scene to the next;
- props and furniture requirements;
- costume requirements;
- lighting effects;
- sound or music;
- anything which may be a health and safety issue;
- anything else which may be a problem.

One way of doing this is to make notes in the script and then transfer these onto a chart, which can be used in discussions and meetings.

CHOOSING THE CREATIVE TEAM

In a producing theatre, the decision as to whether the production is to be directed by the artistic or associate director will already have been made. If it is to be a guest director, they

---

French's Acting Editions

Many play scripts are published by the theatre bookshop Samuel French, and contain lists of requirements about the play, often including a groundplan and a list of cues for each department. They are known as 'French's Acting Editions', and the information is based on the prompt copy of the first professional performance of the play. However, its information should be used sparingly, as it may not have anything to do with the way your director intends to stage the piece.

---

will be approached and contracted by the artistic director or chief executive. A production company will probably have a director in mind from the start of the project, and again they will be contracted by the chief executive. Amateur companies may use the same director (confusingly often called the producer) for each production, or a number of directors from inside or outside the company.

The director will probably have ideas about the person or people they want to use to design the show. They will probably make the initial approach to the designer(s) but it may be the responsibility of the production manager to talk to the designer or their agent when it comes to the matter of fees and production dates.

It can take a surprisingly long time to get a designer on board for a production, mainly because they are not going to accept the work without doing a certain amount of research. They will want to read the play, look at other definite commitments or possible commitments that might clash, meet with the director if they do not know each other well, and discuss the fee. This all takes time, and in their scheduling of the production process, the pro-

Model Box

The designer will have to start by building a model of the theatre or studio to show the basic limits of the building; this is usually done using black card or polyboard sprayed black. It is a time-consuming and expensive process.

You might offer your designer an existing empty model box if you have one, but do not be surprised if this offer is turned down. Many designers find making the model box an ideal way of getting to know the theatre space, and therefore like to build a model box from scratch.

Especially for studios or spaces with adaptable seating, it is a good idea to have model pieces of all the seating blocks, which the designer can use to produce possible seating layouts quickly and easily. This is a good example of production management facilitating other people's work.

duction manager needs to allow time for several designers to turn down the work.

The director and set designer will probably discuss who they would like to light the show, and again, time needs to be allowed to get that person on board, although the basic design process can start without them. The sound designer will also be contracted at this time.

BRIEFING THE CREATIVE TEAM

This is the start of very important relationships for the production manager. Ideally they will be able to arrange a briefing meeting with the whole creative team at the theatre where the show is first to be performed, though they may need to compromise on this, depending on availability. The production manager should make sure that they are as prepared as possible for the first meeting with the director, and particularly the designer.

If the production manager has not worked with the creative team before, an informal lunch usually gets things off to a good start; before moving to an office to discuss details, and into the theatre to look at the space. The theatre world is quite small, and the production manager will probably find at this informal meeting that they and the creative team have worked with the same people, or have seen some of each other's work. With new teams this is a very useful topic of conversation in establishing common ground and knowledge.

Creative teams will be used to working in a variety of theatres, each of which will work in slightly different ways. Members of the team need to receive a lot of information, and it is a good idea to have this in written form, as guidelines. These can give a good deal of information about the theatre or production company and how it works, and what is expected of the creative team.

It is a good idea to include a copy of the guidelines with designers' contracts and make 'working within them' part of the terms of the contract. It can work well to have one overall document with additional pages for the director, set and costume designer, lighting designer and sound designer. It is also a good idea if the guidelines are from the chief executive and/or artistic director as well as the production manager.

During the briefing meeting, the creative team will need to be told or have confirmed:

- what the production budget is, and what has to come out of it;
- the staffing levels (for building the production and for running it), and whether there is a budget for additional staff;
- the first rehearsal, fit-up and first performance dates;
- where the show is rehearsing;
- a rough breakdown of how the time will be used once the show moves into the theatre.

WHAT TO INCLUDE IN DESIGNER GUIDELINES

You should add your own information under each of these headings.
These can be amended to produce guidelines for all other members of the creative team.

BUDGETS - MONEY, STAFF & TIME

Production budget
- What the budget includes
- Your policy on hiring
- Will there be a separate lighting budget
- Paying for any additional staff
- Amount of overtime available during the build period
- Outworkers
- Note that stock items are not charged to the production budget.
- Are model making expenses included
- Travel and accommodation
- Budgeting is also done in terms of time, both for building and fitting up the show.
- Possible work on stage before the fit up?

Staffing for building the show:
- Workshop staff and their capabilities (metal and timber?)
- Paintshop
- Props
- Stage Management (to do the props finds or borrows and paperwork props)
- Wardrobe
- Assistant Designer?
- Length of build period
- Working hours before overtime
- Other matters the staff have to be available for? (training, other shows in production, current show)

Show staffing:
- Lighting board operator
- Sound operator (or is the show being operated '1 man')
- Stage management and any restrictions as to what they can do (eg CSM not to have any Qs)
- Stage technician(s)
- Dresser(s)
- Is there a budget for additional show staff?

TIME DURING PRODUCTION WEEK
- Rough breakdown session by session
- Number of Dress Rehearsals
- Opportunity for notes

ATTENDANCE & MEETINGS
- The dates and times of the major meetings (White card, Production Meetings, Progress Meetings)
- What is needed for each meeting
- First rehearsal and read through
- Other attendance expected (eg number of days per week), final run through and production week
- Checking with production manager at the end of each visit
- Lighting meeting
- Props meeting

STOCK
- What is available (with numbers and sizes) and arrangements for seeing it. Masking, Steeldeck, stage machinery, items of scenery, gauzes, coloured drapes.
- Some information about stock props, furniture and wardrobe items

WHAT IS NEEDED FROM A DESIGNER?
- Groundplan, side elevation, model, furniture plan for stage management(?), (what blank drawings or CAD files will the theatre be supplying)
- technical drawings (or exact reference including dimensions) of all scenery, props and furniture being made)
- Drawings or exact reference including colour of all wardrobe items to be made plus a list of all costumes.

HEALTH & SAFETY
- Their responsibility
- Theatre or Company's Health & Safety Policy
- Codes of Practice
- Risk Assessments for the show
- Fire regulations and use of naked flame
- Other regulations (eg handrails, safety curtain)

GENERAL
- Rehearsals
- Rehearsal notes
- Weekly Production Schedules
- Office space and use of telephone
- First night tickets

Depending on where the meeting is happening, the creative team will also want to have blank drawings of the stage to take away. These should be on paper (for reference), on tracing paper (for drawing the final plan), or on disc if the designer uses a computerized drawing package.

They will also want a tour of the theatre, especially the stage and auditorium, and if there are resident production staff, to meet them as they tour the building. The production manager should introduce every member of staff the creative team meets; they won't remember them, but it makes everyone feel involved, and it also means that people have met before the first production meeting. The production manager should have a staff list and contact details available for the team.

They might point out the work that is going on, so that the creative team gets an idea of the quality of work the staff can achieve.

During the briefing meeting the production manager will want to achieve the following:

- Make sure the creative team understands the scale of the production envisaged by the theatre or production company.
- Give the creative team a rough breakdown of how the theatre anticipates the production budget will be spent. This will give them an indication of how big the show is seen as being from each department's point of view. It also gives a target figure to aim for later, if the costing is badly over budget.
- Agree the dates of future production meetings.

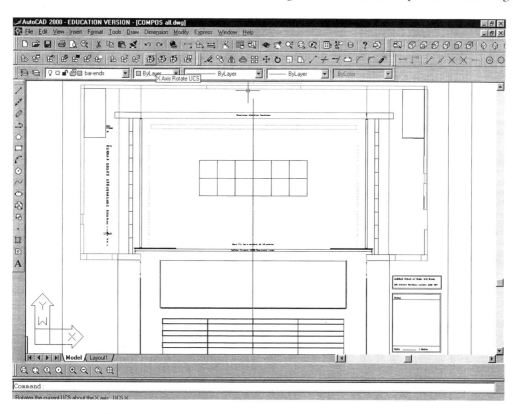

A blank theatre drawing on a computer.

- Discuss what is needed from the team at each of the production meetings.
- Point out what can be done with the theatre – different seating layouts, orchestra pit possibilities, places for entrances and exits.
- Point out any problems to do with the stage – difficult sightlines, reduced wing space, fire or licensing regulations.
- Show the team, or discuss with them, any equipment or stock items that may be of use to the production.
- Note days when designers are committed elsewhere (their non-availability), and discuss how often they will need to attend during the rehearsal and build period. Days when designers are not available should go on the schedule for the show when it is published.
- Agree contracts and fees if they have not yet been finalized.
- Get contact details from the team.

Contacting the Creative Team

You will need to be able to contact the creative team wherever they are, often quite urgently. Make sure that you get telephone, fax, mobile and pager numbers, as well as email and home addresses.

If you do not already have them, you will want details about their agent for contract purposes. Some designers work from home, but some have studios where they base themselves. Get details of these as well.

If they are doing other productions at the same time as yours, you may also want contact details of the theatres where these are happening.

It is a good idea to publish these details for selected people working on the production. However, you should have a system in place to make sure that calls to the creative team are managed by someone (you, your assistant if you have one, or the stage manager) so that they are not constantly interrupted.

You also need to give the creative team details of how they can contact you.

Production Office		Creative Team Contact Details
Production		
		Address
Director		
Home Phone		
Mobile Phone		
Other Phone		
Fax		
e mail		Agent's Address
Agent		
Agent Phone		
Agent Fax		
		Address
Designer		
Home Phone		
Mobile Phone		
Other Phone		
Fax		
e mail		Agent's Address
Agent		
Agent Phone		
Agent Fax		
		Address
Lighting Designer		
Home Phone		
Mobile Phone		
Other Phone		
Fax		
e mail		Agent's Address
Agent		
Agent Phone		
Agent Fax		

The lighting designer will want to meet the chief electrician and have a fairly long discussion with the team about the equipment, the venue, the LX team and their way of working. They will want to have a list of equipment, and a blank lighting plan, and will want to know when the lighting plan is needed.

Initial Design

Designers will start their work on the production by reading the play and listening to the music, if appropriate, so they can come

Left: A form for recording creative team contact details.

A designer's initial sketch for a production of Beggar's Opera. *Designer: Neil Irish.*

up with their initial feelings about the production. They will meet with the director and, if available, the lighting designer to begin to discuss in broad terms what they want the production to look like. They will discuss the period and style in which they want to set the production, and the designer may start to do some research and to produce some sketches.

If the designer has any queries at this stage, or needs further information, they will contact the production manager. They will have a series of meetings with the director, will continue developing the design, and will start building a scale model ready for the first production meeting. This meeting has a variety of names, depending on the organization, but its purpose is the same: it is often called the 'white card model meeting'.

WHITE CARD MODEL MEETING

The purpose of this meeting is to make sure that the design is on track in terms of scale and resources before the designer undertakes the time-consuming work of producing a fully finished model and drawings. The designer will produce a scale model made of unpainted card (hence 'white card model'), but will give an indication or description of some of the paint finishes.

All the creative team should attend this meeting if possible, but certainly the director and designer must be there. The meeting will be chaired by the production manager, and key heads of department (stage management, paintshop, workshop, props, wardrobe, LX and sound) will attend. They should be prepared to offer input in a positive way before the design process is completed, and to cost the proposed design very roughly in terms of time, space and materials. This is to give the creative team an indication of whether they are on track with the scale of the design.

After introductions, the director should give a brief **overview of the production**, including the period in which it has been decided to set it. They should then hand over to the designer to go through the white card model. If the design is over-ambitious, however much too big it seems to be, the production manager should let the designer go right through the model before expressing concern.

Once the **set model** has been presented, there should be the opportunity to go through it in more detail from each department's point of view. HODs should ask questions and decide whether they think the design is feasible or not within available resources. Although they will

White Card Model Meeting Checklist

For the meeting, the **creative team** needs to have produced:
- a white card model;
- a list of costumes needed;
- a list of major props and furniture items;
- a list of special lighting requirements or effects.

The **production manager** needs to have:
- informed the staff that the meeting is happening, and briefed them about the show and available resources;
- made sure that those who need them have copies of the script in advance;
- booked a suitable room;
- produced an agenda.

A white card model (compare with the previous illustration).

Scale

The scale used in most theatres is 1:25 (where metric measurements are used) or 1:24 (½in to the foot, where imperial measurements are used).

All theatre technicians and stage management should be used to working to scale, and will have their own scale rule that converts a scaled measurement to an actual one.

Some designers will want to produce smaller scale models for the white card model meeting, but you should try not to allow this, because if you are used to working at 1:25, a 1:50 model can be very difficult to assess – and you will get a nasty shock when you see the design at 1:25!

have their own thoughts about the design, production managers should support their HODs' points of view, because these are the people who have to produce the work.

As well as the actual building and painting of the set, there needs to be a discussion about how it is to be fitted up, any touring implications, and how scene changes are envisaged. Departments should raise any ideas about items that are in stock, or small changes to the proposed design that would make it considerably easier or cheaper.

After discussing the set, the meeting should move on to discuss **furniture and props**: hopefully the designer will have a list that can be copied and distributed. Again, stock items can be important here. The stage manager should have produced a detailed list from reading the script, and should highlight any specific problems they have spotted, particularly to do with how props need to be used.

If there is a prop-making department, the HOD should give a view on what can be

achieved by them; other items would need to be hired or propped. If there is not a making department, a greater percentage of the requirements will have to be hired; this is usually a stage management responsibility. The production manager may want the departments to estimate the size of budget they will need, based on the props and furniture list. They may also want to arrange for the creative team to see stock items after the meeting so that, if appropriate, they can incorporate them into the finished design.

Wardrobe requirements for the production should be discussed. Again, the creative team should have a list, as should the wardrobe supervisor. Discussions need to take place about what is to be made, either in-house or by freelancers, what might be available from stock, and what can be bought. This should allow the wardrobe supervisor to estimate very roughly the budget they will require.

Once the meeting has dealt with the set, props, furniture and costume, it should move on to **LX and sound** requirements. These are likely to have mainly budgetary implications, rather than space or time, as they will be to do with the hiring of equipment. Again, the production manager may want HODs to estimate the level of budget they think they will require.

By the **end of the meeting** a consensus should have been reached about whether the design is achievable for each department in terms of available resources. If it is too ambitious, a clear indication should be given of how much too big the design is, and the creative team should leave the meeting knowing what they have to do, and what compromises will be necessary to make the design achievable.

Confirmation will be needed as to when the next meeting is (the first production meeting), and what is needed from everyone for that meeting. The designer will need enough time between the white card meeting and the first production meeting to complete the model and

A production meeting in progress.

drawings. If the design was so unachievable that the creative team needs to completely think again, rather than just make modifications, the production manager may need to call another white card model meeting. There needs to be enough time in the overall produc-

tion planning for this to happen if necessary. The production manager should be prepared to be contacted by the creative team after the meeting to be asked further questions, and may even want to instigate this contact, particularly if there are a great many changes to the design to take on board.

Risk Assessments

For production management, work with the creative team on the safety of the show starts at this meeting. You need to start keeping notes of the points discussed and decisions made that will feature in the risk assessment when this is produced. If ideas are being suggested which you believe may be unsafe, you should raise your concerns now so that the design or proposed action can be altered at this early stage.

THE FIRST PRODUCTION MEETING

Again, this meeting may have a different title in each organisation. Its purpose is for the creative team to give production departments all the information they need to cost the show. It should be scheduled long enough before the final production meeting to allow time for departments to cost the design.

Presenting their work to a group of people whom they may not know very well can be a very stressful time for designers. The produc-

79

tion manager should remember this, and should try to make things as easy as possible for them. Meet them before the meeting and make sure they have plenty of time to set up the model, and a suitable table on which to do so. They will probably have travelled a distance, so see if they need refreshment. At the start of the meeting make them feel welcome. Keep all discussion about the design positive, and do not be dismissive about any part of it: a finished model is the result of hours of painstaking work.

The same people should attend the first production meeting as attended the white card model meeting, but because there will be

a finished model, more junior members of departments may be asked to attend, at least for the presentation of the model. Other departments, such as marketing, may also like to attend to see how the production is going to look. If the DSM is on board at this point, he or she should also attend.

The director may wish to repeat or update his overview of the production, and how the design was arrived at. There may also be news on casting. The set and costume designers should give a detailed presentation of their part of the show, and the lighting designer will give details of any major requirements so that they can be costed. Each department should make detailed notes about what it is required to produce. They may wish to arrange a subsequent meeting with members of the creative team.

Minutes of the meeting will need to be produced, and it must be decided (in advance) who is going to be responsible for this: it could be the production manager or an assistant if they have one, or the stage manager. It is a good idea to ask the sound department to record the meeting to make the writing of minutes an easier task.

If there is uncertainty about which department is responsible for an item, or if there are items that several departments will be expected to work on, the production manager should make this clear both at the meeting and in the minutes.

The minutes of the first production meeting will list the requirements from each department for the production, and can form the basis of the costing for the show, or serve as a double check for each department.

The designer must leave the model with the production staff so that it can be used for costing. Production management should arrange to have copies of all drawings made, including at least one for themselves and one for the designer.

First Production Meeting Checklist

For this meeting the **creative team** need to have:
- completed the model
- produced a groundplan and a side elevation of the set in the theatre
- produced scale drawings of everything which is to be made
- finalized the list of costumes needed and produced drawings or reference for all of these
- finalized the list of major props and furniture items, and produced model pieces and drawings for all items being made
- turned the list of special lighting requirements or effects into a list of equipment required.

The **production manager** needs to have:
- set up the meeting as before
- invited any major contractors they intend to use to attend the meeting
- Researched anything they needed to from the white card model (eg, specific regulations, specialist suppliers or craftsmen).

The finished model (compare with the illustrations on pages 76–7).

COSTING THE PRODUCTION

Each department will now cost every item that it is required to produce for the production, based on the model, working drawings and discussions with the creative team. It is important that the costing is done by those who will have to work on the design, as decisions will be made at this stage about how the design is to be realized.

It is also important that departments cost what has been designed, not what they think is feasible or what they would like to make. The time for compromise may come later, but the creative team needs to be able to see the true cost of what they have designed.

Production management should facilitate the costing process by supplying prices when needed, or by agreeing to enter the data from a hand-written costing if production departments lack computer technology or skills. There may be some items that it has been agreed are the responsibility of production management to price, and they will co-ordinate the costing and check that each department has included everything that has been asked for, even if it is coming from stock. Each production manager will decide how they want the costings presented, but it is a good idea to use a spreadsheet. This can be constantly revised, especially at the production meeting where changes and cuts can be made instantly, and the costing total will automatically update.

The costing should show a sub-total for each item needed for the production, a total for

*A departmental
discussion about
a model.*

Minutes of Meetings

These should:

- be produced as soon as possible after the meeting;
- be checked by the production manager before distribution;
- be a summary of the decisions made;
- not include discussion points unless these are relevant to the final decision;
- be in a logical order, though not necessarily in the order they were discussed at the meeting;
- list action points and who needs to take that action, together with the deadline if appropriate;
- include all health and safety items;
- state any deadlines (for instance when costings have to be completed) and when the next meeting is;
- be signed and dated;
- have a distribution list at the bottom.

each department, and a total for the show. It should state what the production budget is, and how much over (or under) the total is, and it should be sent to the creative team a minimum of twenty-four hours before the production meeting. This means that if the show is over budget, they have time to look at the costing; they also have a price for each item. They can then prioritize and decide, for example, that a particular costume may be worth its costing because of its impact in the show, or because of how often it is used, but that a lighting effect does not justify the expense.

Each department should also receive a full copy of the costing. They will check the costing of their part of the production, but they should also check that nothing they are aware of has been omitted, or costed for by another department.

If a show is over budget (and they often are), the production manager and their HODs will have ideas about where savings can be made. The production manager may want to discuss these with the creative team when they send them the costings, or they may want to see what the creative team come up with. This will depend on their relationship.

When sending out the costing, it is worth emphasizing the scale of the problem (if there is one), and also making it clear that cuts or simplifications will have to be made because there is no more budget available.

The production manager and their HODs should also cost the show in terms of other resources: time, people and space. Although a show may be affordable in terms of the production budget, it may take too long to fit up, or paint or light. It may also not be feasible in terms of its size and the amount of storage space needed before it fits up. It may need additional staff to prepare or run it. All of these need to be known so that they can be discussed at the final production meeting and suitable compromises reached.

Contingency Funds

It is vital that an amount of the production budget is kept back as a contingency, perhaps 5 to 10 per cent. However, the existence and extent of this budget should not be revealed to anyone, nor should it be eaten into at the costing, or even the final production meeting stage.

The contingency exists to pay for mistakes that departments may make, changes in prices from those quoted at the costing stage, and for unavoidable additions that come out of rehearsals or during the production of items for the show.

Each department will probably also have its own built-in contingency that may be listed in their costings as 'hardware', 'items from rehearsal', 'contingency for stock cos-

	A	B	C	D	E	F	G	H	I	J
3	SUMMARY			PAINT	£493.57					
4				SCENERY	£3,409.13					
5	BUDGET		£7,500.00	PROP MAKES	£1,138.49					
6				SM PROPS	£670.43					
7				WARDROBE	£2,310.00					
8				LX	£2,196.22					
9				SOUND	£0.00					
10										
11				TOTAL	£10,217.84					
12				BUDGET	£7,500.00					
13				OVER BY	£2,717.84					
14	PAINTSHOP COSTING									
15	ITEM	Description	Unit Cost		COST					
17	Black emulsion	1 x 5 litres	£10.50		£10.50					
18	White emulsion	14 x 5 litres	£10.50		£147.00					
20	Artex	2 x 25kg Bag	£16.31		£32.67					
22	Matt glaze	1 x 5 litres	£20.49		£20.49					
24	Bromabond	1 x 5 litres	£12.06		£12.06					
26	Rosco Leather lake	2@ 5 litres	£70.20		£140.40					
27		2@ 1 litres	£15.85		£31.70					
29	Rosco Velour Black	1@ 1 litre	£8.35		£8.35					
31	Rosco Yellow Ochre	1@ 5 litres	£40.50		£40.50					
33	Rosco Burnt Umber	1@1 litre	£9.90		£9.90					
35	Size				£15.00					
37	SUNDRIES				£25.00					
39	PAINT TOTAL				£493.57					
40										

A costing on a computer.

tumes not fitting' etc. There should also be a contingency in the overtime and freelance and casuals budgets.

THE FINAL PRODUCTION MEETING

This is the most important, and potentially the longest meeting of the production process. At the very latest it should be scheduled a few days before the first rehearsal, and before any production work starts. At the meeting, which must again be accurately minuted, the production manager should:

- confirm all information regarding the production (personnel, design, schedule);
- negotiate cuts to the design if necessary to bring it within time and financial budgets;
- agree who will be responsible for each element of the production;
- discuss and minute any health and safety issues;
- finalize the arrangements for the start of rehearsals;
- clear up any other unresolved items to do with the production.

The full creative team, all production HODs, and all members of the stage management team should attend.

After **introductions** of anyone who was not at the previous meetings, and giving any apologies for absence, it is worth checking that the information from which everyone is working, is up to date. The production manager should check with the creative team that nothing in the design has changed. They should talk about anything that came to light during the costing process – for example, it was discovered that a stock item would not be available for the production – and check with each department that the costings as presented are

accurate. There may be items that have had to be estimated, or are not included in the distributed costing, and these should be pointed out at this stage.

The meeting should then look at the **total costing**. If it is under budget that is excellent, but the production manager should make it clear that the budget is a maximum, not a target, and that it is not necessarily appropriate for items to be added. If, as more often happens, the production is over budget, the production manager should first look to the creative team for possible cuts. This can be one of

Final Production Meeting Checklist

For this meeting the **creative team** need to have:
- looked at and discussed the costings, and come up with suggested cuts or compromises if necessary.

The **production manager** needs to have:
- set up the meeting as before and produced an agenda;
- allowed themselves and others plenty of time for the meeting;
- arranged for the pieces of the model to be brought to the meeting and re-assembled (they will have been taken away by different departments to cost the show);
- discussed the costing and possible cuts with each HOD;
- prepared a list of cuts or compromises that gets the show within budget;
- discussed time, space and personnel implications with each HOD;
- transferred the costing to a laptop, if available;
- made sure there are spare copies of the costings in case anyone has forgotten theirs.

the most difficult parts of a production manager's job, and calls for the utmost diplomacy.

Concerns the production manager or HODs have about time, space or personnel should also be discussed so that these can be addressed as well. It is usually the case that if a production is over its budget it will also be over in terms of other resources, and making financial cuts will also help here. These other resource issues should be returned to once the show is within the production budget.

How the production manager deals with **cuts** on a show that is over budget will depend on the creative team and the production manager's relationship with them. Hopefully the director and designers will respond to promptings, and will already have thought of suitable cuts that will have the minimum impact on the show. If they have, the production manager should go through these department by department and alter the costings as they go so that everyone can be informed of the total figure at the end of their list of cuts.

If the creative team do not have ideas about cuts, the production manager needs to bring some authority to the meeting. Production managers are not magicians, and should not allow themselves to be put in the position where they are expected to find ways of making a design happen for less than the realistic costing. Firstly, they should point out that the production budget is finite and cannot be exceeded; and secondly, that it is at this meeting that cuts have to be made, as the production cannot continue until it is within budget. The production manager should now turn to their own list of possible cuts or compromises, and see if the creative team will agree to any of these.

It can be very stressful for all concerned, but the meeting has to keep going until the show is affordable. It is worth going through the costings department by department and discussing ideas that HODs have had. In extreme

---

Meetings

Production managers spend a lot of time chairing meetings, and there are some basic rules that you should observe to make these more effective.

- Book a suitable room and make sure everyone knows where it is.
- Make arrangements for visitors (for instance, the creative team) to be met and taken to the meeting, and to have refreshments if necessary.
- Produce an agenda and distribute it before the meeting so everyone knows what is to be discussed. Use this as the basis of the meeting.
- Start the meeting by welcoming newcomers and introducing everyone present.
- Keep control of the meeting. Do not allow separate conversations to start: 'Can we keep it to one meeting, please' is a good way of doing this.
- Keep the meeting businesslike and moving on, but allow everyone to contribute.
- Be prepared to arrange a subsequent meeting if there are items to discuss that involve only one or two people.
- At the end of the meeting summarize who has agreed to do what.
- If appropriate, set or confirm the date and time for the next meeting while everyone is still present.

---

cases the production manager may agree to continue with a production slightly over budget (knowing that they have a contingency); or, if they feel further cuts are going to jeopardise the whole production, they may undertake to talk to the management about increasing the budget. Everyone needs to bear in mind that there is probably not the time (or the inclination) to completely re-design the show at this point: it may be only a few days before it

A costing with cuts, as marked at the production meeting.

Scene	Prop Details	SOURCE	COST
Overture	6 Black Torches	Stock	
	6 Long thick candles (approx.1m tall)	Buy	~~£94.26~~
	Church incense burner on chain and church incense	Borrow	*cheaper source*
	Cross on pole	Borrow	
	Chalice and fake hosts	Stock	*+ some stock* £15.71
Act 1 Scene 1	Table (Green Card Table)	Borrow	
	4 chairs	Stock	
	Chess board and pieces (large pieces)	Stock/Borrow	
	~~6 Ammunition boxes @ £20.00 each~~ CUT	Buy ~~Borrow~~	~~£120.00~~
	10 Reconnaissance photos @ £5.00 each	Make	~~£50.00~~
	Papers	Stock *5 only 25.00*	
	Large Field Map	Stock	
	Army Field Wireless	Borrow	
	Crate of Beer bottles (Budweiser)	Borrow	
	6 Guns and pistols in holsters @ £8.75 each	Hire	£61.70
	Bowl of water, towel	Stock	
Act 1 Scene 2	Blindfold(s) (Must be able to see through them)	Make	
Act 1 Scene 3	Microphones and stand	Stock	
	2 Rifles	Stock	
	~~Flag or banner (Awaiting Design)~~ CUT		
Act 1 Scene 4	Prayer mat	Stock	
	Chair	Stock	
Act 1 Scene 5	Knife and scabbard	Hire	£25.00
Act 1 Scene 6	Boomerang Birds or Aeroplanes (silent)	Buy	£9.98
	Bottled beer	Borrow	
	Begging Bowl	Stock	
	Catholic iconography	Stock/Borrow	£50.00
Act 1 Scene 7	Gas Mask	Buy	£15.00
	Pistol and holster for Rinaldo	Stock	
Act 2 Scene 1	Lighter	Stock	
	Taper	Stock	
	Votive Candles	Stock	
Act 2 Scene 4	2 Chairs	Stock	
	Piece of soft rope (cotton)	Stock	
	2 blindfolds	Make	
	Handheld (hurricane lamp)	Stock	
	Bottle of water	Stock	
	Tin cup	Stock	
	Beaded Curtain	Buy	£9.99
Act 2 Scene 7	Knife and scabbard (same as Act 1 Scene 5)		
Act 3 Scene 1	Suitcase	Stock	
	Holy water bottles *10*	Acquire	*Reduced number*
Act 3 Scene 11	~~8~~ 12 kevlar helmets @ £15.00 each	Buy *+ cheaper*	~~£180.00~~ *80.00*
General	5 Doormats @ 90p each	Buy	£4.50
	Sundries		£50.00
STAGE MANAGEMENT PROPS TOTAL			~~£670.13~~

346.88

Estimated Budget. Stage Management Props

---

starts rehearsing, and production staff need to start work or they will run out of time.

The meeting should now return to the question of **other resources**, and see if the cuts and compromises have helped any problems here (or made them worse). Again the production manager needs to negotiate with the creative team until these areas are within budget.

The rest of the meeting should be about the practicalities of **making the show happen**, and the following should be arranged or confirmed:

- A meeting with construction and painting HODs to discuss the order of building the show (the build/paint meeting).
- Progress meetings.
- A detailed props meeting involving the director, designer and stage management and prop-makers (if this did not happen prior to costing the show).
- The rough production week schedule.
- When shopping for fabrics can start (this needs the designer), and when cast measurements can be taken so that wardrobe can start on their work. This can sometimes be before rehearsals start.
- The first day of rehearsals, showing the model to the cast, and measuring them for costumes.
- When the lighting plans are due: the production manager should check that the creative team intend to meet during rehearsals to discuss lighting.
- A date for the parade of costumes and props.
- When items will be available to go into rehearsals – for example specific items of props or furniture, music, shoes.
- designers' availabilities and when departments next need to see them.
- Any special requirements the director has for rehearsals.

The production manager should now raise any **health and safety issues**, and discuss their implications. (This is covered in the next chapter.) Finally, the creative team should be reminded that changes in requirements (particularly additions) after the final production meeting must first be agreed with the production management and the department(s) concerned, and must not increase costs.

The production manager should close the meeting by running through agreed action points, particularly those to do with the revised costing. The designer may well need to make revisions to drawings or model pieces, and should check what each department needs in order to start work on the production. However difficult the meeting has been, it is only the start of the production process, so the production manager should finish it in a positive way.

After the meeting, the minutes and a revised costing need producing and distributing quickly: this will be the definitive list of what each department is to be responsible for producing. Everyone is then ready to start rehearsing and building the production. However, before looking at this in detail, we must consider one specific aspect of a production manager's job: their responsibility for ensuring the safety of everyone involved in the production. This work and the knowledge needed are so important that the whole of the next chapter is devoted to it.

5 WORKING SAFELY

A theatre is, by its very nature, a dangerous place. There are instances of theatre technicians being killed in accidents at work in recent years, and many other less serious accidents which have nevertheless seriously affected people's lives and ability to work.

In a theatre there are many areas where people are expected to work at heights, use powerful machinery and move heavy pieces of scenery and equipment. Light levels are often reduced both on and off stage, productions often call for unusual and potentially dangerous effects, and long hours of work are the norm. There is a large amount of electrical equipment in use, which often needs to be mobile and will also produce heat. A large number of people are gathered in a relatively small space, and performers may have a lot of nervous adrenalin, which may make them react unpredictably.

A production manager is directly or indirectly responsible for ensuring the safety of everyone involved in the production. This whole area is usually known as 'health and safety'. It can be seen as a chore involving a lot of paperwork and telling people that they cannot do things. In fact it is a system for:

- producing a safe working environment;
- protecting all those working on the production from harm;
- protecting the theatre or theatre company from litigation or adverse publicity;

- protecting everyone from feelings of personal responsibility should there be an accident;
- ensuring that no one is asked to do anything which could affect their health now or in the future.

Having to assess the risk involved in every aspect of the production, and then write down

HSE
Health & Safety
Executive

HEALTH AND SAFETY LAW

What you should know

Your health, safety and welfare at work are protected by law.

Your employer has a duty to protect you and keep you informed about health and safety.

You have a responsibility to look after yourself and others.

If there is a problem, discuss it with your employer or safety representative, if there is one.

A health and safety poster.

the result of the assessment and the safety measures put in place, ensures that all risks have been considered, eliminated or reduced to acceptable levels.

The basis of health and safety legislation is that every employee (and self-employed person) must:

- Take reasonable care for their own health and safety and that of other people who may be affected by their acts or omissions at work.
- Co-operate with the employer so far as is necessary to perform any duty safely, or comply with any requirements imposed as a result of any law.
- Use the equipment allocated to them in accordance with any training given, and comply with the relevant regulations and codes of practice.
- Not interfere with, or misuse, anything that is provided for the health, safety and welfare of themselves and fellow members of staff.
- Report to the employer any serious danger or shortcomings in the employer's health and safety precautions. Every employee should report any work situation or practice that in their opinion represents a serious and immediate danger to health and safety either to themselves, to colleagues or the public.

HEALTH AND SAFETY POLICY

Each professional theatre or theatre organization must by law have a health and safety policy that states its commitment to health and safety, and the arrangements and responsibilities for:

- assessing risks;
- training;
- maintenance of the workplace and equipment;
- working conditions (heating, lighting, cleanliness, eating, washing and toilet facilities).

The company will undertake to comply with legislation to do with:

- work equipment;
- manual handling;
- computer work stations (display screen equipment);
- safety wear (personal protective equipment);
- electricity;
- substances hazardous to health;
- reporting of accidents or illness;
- first-aid provision, including training the correct number of suitably qualified staff and maintaining fully stocked first-aid boxes.

The document will state the lines of responsibility for the implementation of the health and safety policy. This usually starts with the board of directors, and runs via the chief executive (to ensure that budgets are available), the production manager (for backstage and technical areas), theatre manager (for front of house areas and members of the public), to heads of department, individual employees and freelance workers including actors. Larger organizations will have a health and safety officer or department who will monitor the organization of health and safety, and be available for consultation.

The theatre's health and safety policy is a public document, and a summary of it should be on display for all employees to see. The production manager may wish to issue it, or a précis version, to the staff and to visiting designers, freelancers and companies as part of a health and safety handbook that will also include all codes of practice. Stage management should include the most important points in their 'welcome pack' for the performers.

Even amateur companies that do not employ staff should still be working safely and taking all reasonable care. If they hire a professional theatre, they will be expected to observe the theatre's health and safety policy.

RISK ASSESSMENTS

The way that health and safety is implemented is by carrying out risk assessments and producing codes of practice for each activity. It is the production manager's responsibility to carry out and publish a risk assessment for each production. Work on this should start at the very beginning of the production process, from the time of first reading the script, and they must continue to work on it and monitor its use until the production has closed.

Two types of risk assessment need to be carried out: one on the premises or place where the work is being carried out, and one on the tasks undertaken. The way of carrying out either type of assessment is the same, and is best done by the staff working in each department and those managing them. They should answer the following questions, in this order:

1 What are the component parts of the tasks or premises?
2 What are the possible hazards?
3 Who is at risk?
4 What are the existing controls?
5 How severe could the harm be?
6 How likely is the hazard to happen?
7 What is the risk rating? This is done by looking at *severity* against *likelihood* on a matrix.
8 What controls are needed?
9 How are these going to be implemented?

Most organizations have forms to fill in when completing a risk assessment, with spaces provided for answers to all the questions. A production manager with responsibility for health and safety needs to fully understand these questions, and will be involved in implementing, carrying out and monitoring many of the assessments. Here

HEALTH AND SAFETY RISK ASSESSMENT FORM							
Title of the Task				Ref. No			
Location				Assessor Name(s)			
Activity/Plant/ Materials	Hazard	Persons at Risk	Existing controls and Codes of Practice	Risk Rating			Proposed Controls or Action required
				Severit	Likeliho	Rating	
			Signature(s):			Date Completed:	

An example of a blank risk assessment form.

is more detail about each of the questions indicated above:

1 What are the component parts of the tasks or premises?

Each building should be split into its different rooms or areas, and each assessed separately for the potential hazards it contains, and for the equipment that is in it. Each major task – for example, putting on a show – should be split into its separate tasks: this will produce a long list.

2 What are the possible hazards?

A hazard is defined as something with the potential to cause harm, and harm is anything

Codes of Practice

Although each show is different, many of the tasks are the same, or have similarities. Risk assessments for many of the activities you and your staff need to carry out for a show may already have been done. These could include using access equipment, using workshop equipment, and firing pyrotechnics on stage.

If you are working in a producing theatre, you can have codes of practice that are part of the way each department and individual is expected to work, and which only need to be mentioned on a production risk assessment. You do, however, need to check that nothing about the production alters the effectiveness of these codes of practice.

The codes of practice should be given to all new employees, casuals or freelancers, and their HOD should train them in their use. You must get them to sign for the code of practice and the training, and must keep this information on file as proof that the employee has been given instruction.

from slight injury to death, including causing ill health. There are at least seventeen hazards that need to be considered; these include:

- electricity;
- entrapment or entanglement;
- falling objects;
- falls from height;
- fire;
- flying particles;
- heat or hot surfaces;
- human factors;
- impact or collision;
- light levels;
- manual handling;
- noise and vibration;
- sharp objects;
- slips, falls and trips;
- substances;
- water;
- work-related upper limb disorders (or repetitive strain injury).

3 Who is at risk?

This should be a list of employees at risk (by job title) and also include visitors, members of the public, the creative team and performers if appropriate.

4 What are the existing controls?

This section will list things like routine maintenance, safety features installed on machines or designed as part of the building, training, and existing codes of practice.

5 How severe could the harm be?

There are several ways of describing this. Some organizations give the severity a number, between 1 and 5, where 1 is very slight and 5 is extreme. Others use clearly defined words, and this is the method we will be looking at in more detail.

Consider each hazard and ask how severe would be the harm that it could cause. This could be defined as **slight**, meaning that it could cause minor injury; **moderate**, meaning that it might result in three or more days off work; or **extreme**, meaning it could cause death or a disabling injury/illness.

Consider the **reasonably foreseeable severity**. It is possible to think of a scenario where the smallest accident, for example a splinter, can result in death – but this is not helpful in carrying out risk assessments.

6 How likely is the hazard to happen?

Again it is possible to use the number method where 1 is very unlikely and 5 is very likely. Using the word method, we can break this down into **likely** (the hazard is not controlled at all), **unlikely** (there are some protective measures in place but they are inadequate) and **highly unlikely** (the hazard is under tight controls).

7 What is the risk rating?

To calculate this it is necessary to look at the **severity** and **likelihood** on a matrix. This matrix uses words, but it can be done by using numbers, and get a number result between 1 and 25. There would then need to be a definition of the level of action to be taken for each number or range of numbers.

Risk Assessment Matrix			
	Severity		
	Slight	Moderate	Extreme
Highly unlikely	Trivial	Low	Medium
Unlikely	Low	Medium	High
Unlikely	Medium	High	Intolerable

(L I K E L I H O O D)

The risk rating defines the action to be taken. Health and safety legislation uses the phrase '**where reasonably practicable**', which means if the risk is low, there is no requirement to spend large amounts of time or money in reducing it further; but if the risk is very high, every effort should be made to reduce it.

A **trivial** rating means that it is not necessary to take any action or keep any records.

A **low** rating means that it is not necessary to have any additional controls. Monitoring is required to ensure that the controls are maintained, and the theatre may like to consider a solution or improvement that has no significant cost.

A **medium** rating means that efforts should be made to reduce the risk, but not at huge financial cost. Risk reduction should be implemented within a stated time.

A **high** rating means work should not be started until the risk has been reduced. Considerable resources may have to be allocated to reduce the risk. Where the risk involves work in progress, urgent action should be taken.

An **intolerable** risk means that work must not be started or continued until the risk has been reduced. If it is not possible to reduce the risk even with unlimited resources, work has to remain prohibited.

8 What controls are needed?

A decision is now needed on what to do to reduce the risk.

The best thing to do is to **remove** the hazard completely. Ask the question *do we actually need to do the task that gives rise to the risk*. In theatre the answer is often 'yes', although there may be other ways of achieving the same result.

The next best is to make the particular environment a **safe place** by introducing measures

Carrying out Risk Assessments

You will find risk assessments much easier to carry out if you do them with a colleague or group of colleagues. Risk assessment is subjective, particularly when it comes to scoring degrees of harm and likelihood, and someone else's opinion as a 'sounding board' can be very useful. You will also then have help in devising and implementing safe systems of working and codes of practice, and these will not be seen as being imposed by you.

such as using safer machinery, or putting physical guards in place.

The least effective control is **safe people**. This includes issuing protective equipment, providing additional training, posting notices and, in theatre, making sure hazardous moments are rehearsed.

Before any controls are put in place, it is necessary to go back to question 5 ('How severe could the harm be?') and redo the risk assessment, assuming the proposed controls are in place. Provided this reduces the risk to an acceptable level, the proposed measures can be implemented.

9 How are these going to be implemented?

The proposed measures need to be written down, together with who is responsible for carrying them out, and when they will be carried out. It should also be stated when the risk assessment is to be reviewed: this can be after any period of time, though usually not more than a year. For a show, however, it may be necessary to review it soon after the production has opened, and then at regular intervals.

HEALTH AND SAFETY LEGISLATION

Each country will have its own general legislation and specific regulations that apply to theatres and the activities that take place within them. Production managers need to be familiar with all these documents, and fully aware of their implications and requirements. Some of the specific legislation is listed in Appendix II.

Building-based production managers, especially if they are unlucky enough to have an accident in their theatre, are likely to get a visit from an official who is responsible for enforcing health and safety legislation. In the UK this is usually an employee of the Health & Safety Executive, but the responsibility is sometimes delegated to the Environmental Health Department of the local council. Theatres also need to satisfy the local licensing authority and the fire authority, and these two authorities will want to make an inspection before each production opens.

All three organizations are likely to make annual inspections, and they will also visit if the theatre has a particular problem or query. They can also make spot checks, and by law must be allowed onto the premises to do so. If the theatre does get a visit, the officials will not start by looking round the building, but will visit an office, probably the production office, to look at all the paperwork. As well as the health and safety policy document itself, they can – and will – ask to see up-to-date records of:

- all general and production risk assessments;
- any accidents (the Accident Book);
- first-aid arrangements and training;
- noise assessments;
- testing of all electrical equipment (PAT testing);
- the testing of emergency lighting;
- manual handling assessments of all tasks that involve people lifting things;
- assessments of all computer workstations, including desks and chairs;

- staff training, especially in health and safety, and in using equipment;
- the issuing and checking of protective equipment;
- the issuing of codes of practice;
- the theatre's evacuation procedures;
- fire drills;
- routine maintenance and safety inspections of machinery, plant and fire-fighting equipment;
- the testing of water supplies;
- cleaning schedules;
- insurance inspections of lifts and lifting equipment (which includes all flying in the theatre);
- the hours of work under national or international Working Time Directives.

Raked Stages

Anything in the theatre that slopes is known as 'being raked'. Some older theatres were built with permanently raked stages, and steeper rakes are often built for specific productions.

A raked stage presents particular health and safety problems, which need addressing early on in the production process. It is an Equity requirement that anyone working on a raked stage (performers and stage management) should receive training from a suitably qualified person on how to move safely on a rake without injuring themselves. This includes their being set exercises to do before and after working on a rake.

A raked stage also produces particular hazards with regard to access equipment, which will particularly affect focusing. It may be necessary to use a moveable 'anti-rake' to give a flat floor for using a tallescope or genie. Focusing time will be greatly increased.

Responsibility for Health and Safety

The production manager is likely to have a clause about their responsibility in the job description, but they should not feel that they are the only person thinking or caring about health and safety. They should be supported by their management who should:

- make time and money available for training
- make budgets available for maintaining or replacing equipment
- bring a culture of working safely to the whole organization.

If there are serious problems the production manager can also expect to be supported by the theatre's insurance policies and disciplinary procedures. HODs also have a major responsibility to supervise the work of members of their department, and to ensure that they work safely and practise good housekeeping.

MANAGING RISK ON PRODUCTIONS

Assessing, and if possible eliminating or reducing the risk on productions, starts from when the production manager first reads the script. The chart (*see* page 96) itemizes what they need to consider and do with regard to health and safety at every point in the production.

At the beginning of the production process, the production manager will be identifying possible problem areas and making sure that these are taken on board by the creative team. As with everything relating to health and safety, records must be kept, and the production manager should take notes of every conversation or meeting that involves a discussion or decision about potentially dangerous parts of the production.

It is best for the production manager to start work on the risk assessment as soon as they can. They need to be sure that work does not start on any part of the production before the risk assessment has been produced. The

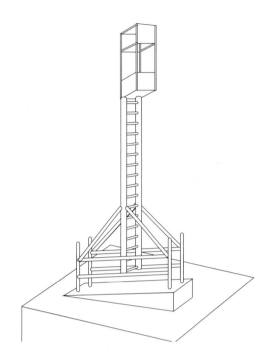

The principle of an anti-rake.

key moments for having risk assessments in place are:

- when starting to build the production;
- at the start of rehearsals;
- the fit-up;
- the technical rehearsal.

It is easiest to issue a separate risk assessment for each of these areas of activity. This means there does not have to be a complete risk assessment of the whole production early in the process, and that things which come out of rehearsal, or which are altered in the design, can be incorporated without having to re-issue the whole risk assessment.

Once work starts on the production, the production manager will be monitoring the work and making sure that everyone is working safely, observing both the codes of practice and the risk assessment. If they find people are *not* working safely or are ignoring agreed codes of practice, unless it is a serious situation, it is best dealt with gently at first: a quiet reminder to individuals or to an HOD may suffice. It also reminds staff that the production manager will be monitoring their work, and that they expect codes of practice and the risk assessment to be followed. If problems persist, there are more formal disciplinary routes that can be followed.

At this time training may need to be arranged for staff, perhaps including the production manager, if there are new substances, equipment or techniques being used on a production. Attendance at training sessions should be recorded by having staff sign an attendance sheet, and details should be kept on each member of staff's personal file.

The Licensing Visit

At some point before the production opens, the licensing authority and fire officer will want to visit the theatre to make sure that the production complies with their conditions. This should be arranged well in advance, to take place at a suitable time during the technical or dress rehearsal period, and the production manager should ensure that they, their stage manager and chief electrician are available during the visit. It is important for the production manager to build up a relationship of mutual trust with the licensing authority and fire officer. This can be done by consulting them for advice at an early stage, if there are areas that may present problems, and by briefing them before they come for the visit. The production manager will also be trusted more if they carry out instructions promptly, and do not attempt to hide anything from the authorities.

The visiting inspectors will want to look at the structural design and construction of the set, and have proof that it is made of flameproof materials (assuming that this is a requirement of the licence). Some flameproof

95

Point in the production process	What the production manager needs to consider	What the production manager needs to do.
When first reading the script	Any hazardous moments mentioned in the text or stage directions	Note the moments for later discussion
When briefing the creative team	Ensuring that the Creative Team understand their responsibility towards Health and Safety	Fully brief the Creative Team and discuss any concerns from reading the script. Issue guidelines as part of the contracts, which include all regulations and relevant codes of practice. Perhaps issue a précis version of the Health and Safety policy
At the white card model meeting	Any hazards which the design creates in its preparation or use. How any hazardous moments in the text or stage directions are being addressed.	Note all Health and Safety points discussed and any decisions reached
At the first production meeting	How any concerns from the White Card Model have been addressed. Has the finished design presented any more problems.	Note all Health and Safety points discussed and any decisions reached
At the second production meeting	How any concerns from the first Production Meeting have been addressed. Any Health and Safety issues which departments wish to raise	Note all Health and Safety points discussed and any decisions reached as a specific agenda item which gets minuted
In producing the production risk assesment	All issues discussed to date. Everything that needs to happen in the show and in preparing it	Go through every task, assess the risk and write it down, as detailed earlier in this chapter. Publish the risk assessment.
In publishing the production risk assesment	That they can prove that everyone concerned received a copy of the risk assessment	Produce a distribution list. Everyone should sign it for the risk assessment
When considering the build and paint schedule	Any tasks which should be carried out in isolation or which will produce specific hazards	Make sure these are scheduled at the appropriate time
In rehearsals	That rehearsals are taking place safely and that any action which could be dangerous is noted, discussed and assessed	Delegate responsibility to the DSM to make sure rehearsals are safe. They should note any concerns for discussion at the progress meeting, or sooner if more urgent.
At fight rehearsals	That these rehearsals take place safely	Employ a competent fight director and make sure that Stage Management run the rehearsals safely
At the final run through	Observe all hazardous moments in the show which have already been assessed and make sure there are none which have been missed.	Discuss any concerns with the director and note any action or changes agreed
When ordering materials	Whether the materials have been used before. Whether they are the safest materials for the job	Obtain COSHH data sheets if material is new. Carry out risk assessment on the new material and, if necessary issue Code of Practice
When planning the fit up and production week	The safest way of carrying out all the work involved.	Hold a briefing meeting.
At the briefing meeting prior to the fitup	That everyone knows what is expected of them during the fit up	Issue a detailed schedule for the fit up stating who will be doing what
During the fit up and focussing	That work is being carried out safely and that the risk assessment is being followed	Monitor the work throughout, especially work going on at heights and that people are wearing protective gear when necessary. Make sure people take breaks
At the tour of the set prior to the technical rehearsal	That the acting company will be able to work safely on the set	Delegate the Stage Manager to take the company around the set and point out safety features and hazards. Make sure the company know that they should report anything which they consider to be dangerous
Throughout the technical rehearsal	That work is being carried out safely and that the risk assessment is being followed	Monitor the work throughout. Stop the action before any known hazardous moment and if anything dangerous is occurring. Work with the Director in making sure everything is used safely and as intended
During the licensing visit	That the licensing authority are happy with all aspects of the production	Produce a list of items the licensing officer needs to know about. Note any action the licensing officer wants carrying out and make sure that it happens
Before each performance	That the theatre is properly prepared for the performance	Make sure that the stage is swept, mopped or hoovered (and that records are kept). Schedule time for fight rehearsals and a fire drill before each performance.
After each performance	That any dangerous occurrences are noted	Make sure that a show report is produced and published and that all necessary action or maintenance is carried out
During the run	That the production remains safe	Make sure that relevant departments, particularly stage and electrics, carry out regular safety checks and that records are kept of these
At the get out	That this will run safely	Prepare a running order for the get out, distribute this and brief people on their

---

Notes for Licensing Visit for 'This Production' at This Theatre

1. The scenery consists of a permanent set of standard flattage construction – flameproof 4mm ply covered in flameproof scenic cotton canvas. 4mm ply is flameproof stamped, delivery note available for canvas.
2. There are a number of matching cushions and drapes which have been made for the production. The fabric has been flame proofed using 'Flamecheck'. A sample piece is available for you to test during your visit.
3. There is one large flown flat, weight 155kg. This is flown on rated cables (4 lines), shackles and bottle screws. Test certificates (batches) available for inspection.
4. The counterweight system is rated at 400kg per bar and is inspected every 6 months. Reports available for inspection.
5. Actors are on stage when this piece flies in but are rehearsed to be at least 2 metres away at the time.
6. There is a fire drill prior to opening the house for each performance
7. The safety curtain will be lowered at the interval
8. Smoking in the production is as follows:
   1) Cigarette lit with match DSR and extinguished SR in ashtray. Lit for 3 minutes
   2) Cigarette lit with lighter DSL and extinguished DSL in ashtray. Lit for 3 minutes
   3) Cigarette lit with lighter DSL and extinguished DSL on floor by foot. Lit for 1 min
9. We have already discussed the issue of the requirement for the use of 50 candles in this production, and you have approved in principal. The details are as follows: Candles are lit on a large table by stage management and crew during a scene change and extinguished by singers at end of show. Lit for 20 minutes. A nominated fire officer will be in attendance with appropriate fire fighting equipment. The candles are mounted on flame proof (class 1) boards. We propose to demonstrate this moment to you during your visit.
10. A Rosco 1500 smoke machine will be used at 2 points during the production. We intend to demonstrate these to you during your visit.

An example of a document produced for a licensing visit.

---

materials are marked with a stamp, but for others it will be necessary to have written proof from the manufacturer. This information may be on the invoice or delivery note, and a copy should be available for the inspectors to keep on their file.

The inspectors should also be given a copy of the risk assessment, and a detailed list of the use of naked flame, smoke machines, weapons or pyrotechnics. These will have to be set up and demonstrated, together with any hazardous moments or stunts.

The production manager should also discuss with the visiting inspectors the safety features in place for the production, and when the

OPPOSITE: **When health and safety is considered during the production process.**

safety curtain is to be used. They may want to have a demonstration of light levels backstage and emergency lighting in public areas.

Rehearsals

Stage management are responsible for ensuring that the rehearsal room is suitable for the activities being carried out, and that the director is working in a safe way. They should particularly monitor how moments or actions that have already been noted as hazardous are dealt with. Any concerns should be referred to the production manager, and should be noted on rehearsal notes for discussion at the next progress meeting. The final run-through is an opportunity to check that all is well, and that the production as rehearsed complies with the risk assessment; but the production manager

Rehearsing a hazardous moment of a show in the rehearsal room.

may want to anticipate problems by going to rehearsals when a particular moment is being rehearsed for the first time.

The Fit-Up

Prior to the fit-up the production manager should hold a briefing meeting with all permanent staff who will be working on it (it is not usually possible to involve casual staff in this meeting). They should already have received the risk assessment, and this should be discussed at the meeting, as should the running order for the fit-up. Staff should be allowed to raise any questions, and they should be aware of what is expected of them from the health and safety point of view, particularly that they need to bring and use their personal protective equipment, and that they should encourage everyone to work safely.

During the fit-up the production manager will want to ensure that work is being carried out safely. They should monitor and enforce codes of practice and methods of working that have been agreed in the risk assessment. All staff should be aware of what is going on around them, and should be communicating with each other; this is particularly important when moving heavy pieces of scenery or flying bars in or out. The production manager should be co-ordinating the fit-up and making sure that everything is safe before moving on to the next task.

The Technical Rehearsal

Just as with almost every other aspect of a production, the technical rehearsal is a key time for health and safety. It is the first time the company are on stage with the set, and as every moment will be worked through, every hazard will be exposed. It is important to emphasize the necessity for safety from the start.

Again, as with other aspects of the show, the tech is not the time to start making up the risk assessment. Everyone involved, from the director down, should be aware of, and be rehearsing what has been agreed in the risk assessment. If it has been agreed that, because of the hazards involved, a particular piece of action is to happen in a particular way, this is not the time to change it, nor is it the time for

technicians to decide to rig or operate an effect in a different way.

Immediately before the start of the tech, stage management, having first checked it through with the production manager, should take the company on a tour of the set, onstage and offstage. They should point out all safety features and hazards, as well as the way things work, and should allow the actors to ask questions. It should be emphasized that, if performers believe themselves to be in danger during

---

Loading, Unloading and Flying Bars

Dealing with counterweight bars when they are being loaded and unloaded is a potentially hazardous operation. There needs to be very good communication between the stage and the fly floor as to when a bar is flying in, when it is safe to load or unload bars or weights and when a bar is ready to be flown out. The work should not be hurried.

The sequence is as follows:

• if striking the previous show as part of the turn round, all cables from the previous rig unplugged
• make sure the bar is free to fly in
• bar called in by chief LX and flown in by fly crew
• bar clamped with rope clamp
• cradle de-weighted by crew on loading gallery
• LX crew told bar is de-weighted and can be unloaded
• equipment de-rigged and moved to new location or stored if not needed
• if using pre wired bar, new location for this identified and empty bar called and flown in and clamped
• pre-wired bar transferred (rigging gear checked)
• empty bar called and flown out
• if appropriate, new LX bar rigged (it may be better to de-rig all bars before starting to re-rig)
• once bar rigged instruction given to loaded the cradle.
• loading gallery crew load the number of weights listed on the hanging plot and tell flyman when this is done
• flyman will check that the bar is in balance and ask for weights to be added or removed as needed
• while loading is going on the LX crew 'flash out' (This is a check that every lantern is working by plugging each plug which runs off the end of the bar into a working socket. By referring to the plan LX can then label the plug top with the circuit number, which saves time when they need to plug up and also help with fault finding)
• just before it flies out, final safety check, by a senior member of the LX team, that each lantern is rigged safely, the hook clamp is tight, each lantern has a secondary means of support (safety bond) fitted and that all accessories are also safely rigged
• bar called out
• bar flown high enough so as not to get in the way of fitting up the set later
• cables hauled out of the way, usually onto the fly floor
• no need to plug them up yet, this can be done at a later stage when other things are happening on stage.

The sequence of loading and unloading flying bars during the rigging of LX bars.

the tech, they should stop and not continue until they are happy that the hazard has been made safe. This particularly applies to having enough light to see what they are doing.

During the technical rehearsal, the production manager should never allow the action to run straight into a dangerous moment. When it gets close to such a point in the show they should:

- stop the rehearsal;
- go onstage and talk through the action with the director, performers, stage management and technicians;
- remind everyone of where they need to be (or more importantly, where they should *not* be);
- remind everyone of what they need to do;
- have technicians demonstrate in full light what is going to happen;
- have stage management and technicians set back, and attempt to run that particular moment or sequence.

As with all aspects of the show, the sequence should be repeated until it is as the director wants it, and it can be achieved safely every time.

Scary Moments

If there is any action about which a performer is particularly nervous, it is worth rehearsing it first away from the technical rehearsal situation and with a minimum number of people around. This particularly applies to people being flown or using guns.

It is important that everyone is disciplined about all aspects of their work, but particularly that, during potentially hazardous moments in a production, they always carry out the same actions at the same time and in the same place.

When it is discovered how things actually work at the technical rehearsal, it may be necessary to make adjustments to the risk assessment to reflect what is actually being done. Any changes should only be agreed provided they do not increase the risk to those involved, be it performer, technician or audience member. It should also be appreciated by all concerned, and especially by creative teams, that at this stage it may not be possible to change some decisions taken during the design and building of a production, and that original intentions and risk assessments will have to be followed.

Dress Rehearsals and Performances

A dress rehearsal is a performance without an audience, therefore from a health and safety point of view dress rehearsals and performances are treated as the same thing. It is important that all pre-show safety checks are made and recorded, and that this includes sweeping, mopping or vacuuming the stage floor as necessary. All machinery should be checked for safe working, and it is worth having a tick box sheet so that these checks can be recorded for every performance.

Time should be scheduled to rehearse any fight – in the correct set and lighting state – and any other moments that it was agreed needed rehearsing before each performance. For their own safety, the company, and particularly dancers, will have a physical warm-up to avoid pulling muscles or hurting themselves in other ways.

A fire drill should also be carried out before 'opening the house' (that is, letting the audience into the theatre). Depending on the procedure in the particular theatre, this should involve stage management (to make the announcement and drop the safety curtain), the lighting board operator (to switch on house lights and working lights), and the front-of-house staff (to open the exit doors). Each member of the show staff will probably have areas of the theatre to check, and a central point to which to report. Records should again be kept of having carried out the fire drill.

After the show any accidents, dangerous occurrences or items that need repair or replacement should be noted on the show report. Stage management should talk any problems through with the performers or technicians concerned.

The Get-Out

As with the fit-up, this should be planned out and discussed in advance, for reasons of both safety and efficiency. A meeting should be held to discuss who is doing what, and in what order, and to talk over any safety issues; if appropriate, this can be combined with the fit-up meeting for the next show. Again, it should be noted as part of the process of managing risks on a production.

MANAGING RISK IN A BUILDING

Building-based production managers will have a responsibility for making sure that all the technical theatre areas of the building are free from hazards, and are maintained as safe places to work. How this happens, and specifically what records are kept, should again be documented in the theatre's health and safety policy document. This should record room dimensions and space, and the number of people working in each area. It should also list the toilet and washing facilities – the regulations stipulate that the number of toilets required is calculated according to the number of people in the building – and the arrangements for the provision of drinking water, rest and eating facilities.

It should outline the theatre's systems for:

• the maintenance of the workplace, all equip-

Reporting forms (see page 104).

101

CODE OF PRACTICE	**Theatre Production Office**

Activity	Using cross cut saw	revised 20/10/2001

Location   Scenic Workshop

Staff involved   Members of the following departments once trained:
Workshop, Props, Maintenance, Electrics, Stage, Production Office
Users must be over 18 years of age

1. Approved Tasks:

• cross cut sawing lengths of timber
• cutting narrow pieces of board
• occasional use as a mitre saw

2. Before Use:

• do not use the machine if any checks are unsatisfactory
• enter in the log any faults damage or maintenance carried out
• disconnect machine from mains before adjusting or dismantling
• ensure dust extractor is running and that vent is open
• check guard is secure and undamaged
• visual check on fence for damage and security
• check that height of blade is set correctly
• check any tools for maintenance or adjustment have been removed from the machine
• check floor around the machine is clear of trip hazards
• check bench is clear of obstructions
• ensure on/off buttons are accessible
• use support for end of timber if protruding from bench
• push the saw right back and hold it there before starting the motor
• allow the machine to speed up before cutting the first piece

3. During Use

• concentrate on the task
• hold work piece firmly against fence
• keep hands away from blade
• do not pull saw too quickly, let the machine do the work
• make sure you are in control of the movement of the machine
• do not leave machine running unattended
• if timber gets behind machine, leave in position, turn machine off immediately and wait for blade to stop before removing timber.

4. After Use:

• ensure machine is switched off
• sweep up any mess produced
• put offcuts in bin or rack
• reset machine if height or angle altered
• close dust extractor vent
• empty dust extractor after major amounts of cutting

CODE OF PRACTICE (Continued)

5. Weekly checks:

- to be recorded in log.
- disconnect machine from mains before adjusting or dismantling
- check guard is secure and undamaged
- visual check on electric cable and plug
- check visible parts for correct operation and function
- check that moving parts operate freely and there are no breakages
- check ventilation openings are free and clean
- check that all other parts are correctly installed
- check that all factors affecting the operation of the machine are in order
- check that the saw does not roll forwards
- check that fence is secure and undamaged
- check that bench top is secure and undamaged

6. Noise:

- this machine is noisy when being used. (102.1 dB(A)).
- the operator must wear ear protection unless performing a 1 off task.
- other staff in the area may choose to wear ear protection.

7. P.P.E. and Clothing:

- clothing should not be loose or likely to be caught in the machine
- long hair should be tied back or in a hat
- staff must wear eye protection
- staff may wish to wear gloves
- respirator must be worn if cutting quantities of MDF

An example of a code of practice for a crosscut saw.

ment and systems, and reporting of defects;
- the electrical testing of portable appliances;
- controlling ventilation and temperature;
- cleaning and disposing of waste;
- lighting, including the maintenance of emergency lighting;
- the use of computer workstations and seating;
- the condition of floors and traffic routes;
- the safety and maintenance of windows and doors;
- the provision of first aid.

There should then be a risk assessment completed for each room, which will include looking at every task undertaken in each area, and every piece of machinery. Where risks are low and similar tasks are undertaken in a number of rooms – for instance, offices or dressing rooms – there can be a generic risk assessment.

In more hazardous environments, especially places such as workshops where a lot of machinery is used, the risk assessment needs to be more detailed and will probably include a **code of practice** for the use and maintenance of each piece of machinery. There will also be codes of practice for each task undertaken.

Introducing codes of practice may seem to be a daunting task, and it is, unless tackled logically area by area, machine by machine and task by task. It is advisable to start with a chart that breaks down the technical areas into sections, and then identifies each machine and task in each section. Again, those working in each area or using each piece of equipment should be involved, because in this way they will feel they have an 'ownership' of the final code of practice, and are therefore more likely to follow it.

Risk assessments for the building are approached in the same way as for productions. Those carrying out the assessment should have a standard form, and should work their way through the sequence outlined earlier in this chapter (*see* Risk Assessments), or the version of it that their company uses.

In any organization there must be a system for reporting accidents, incidents or near-misses, hazards that could lead to accidents in the

future, and items that require maintenance to prevent them becoming hazards in the future. All staff should be encouraged to report these, using standard forms.

It should be clear who should be given the completed forms for investigating accidents or near-misses, for making recommendations to prevent re-occurrences, and for checking that these recommendations are carried out. Certain accidents may need reporting to government bodies if they involve more than three days off work, admission to hospital, broken limbs or death. Production managers should make sure they understand the legislation regarding accident reporting, and that proper records are kept.

It is equally important to know who is responsible for dealing with any hazards that are reported, and any maintenance that is requested, for keeping records about these, and checking that the necessary work is completed.

SIGNIFICANT HAZARDS IN THE THEATRE

Although all possible hazards should be considered in any risk assessment, there are some that, due to the nature of the work, are more likely to occur in a theatre than others. Production managers should be particularly aware of these, and know how best to deal with them. All of these have specific legislation that applies to them, and it cannot be stressed too strongly that production managers must be familiar with this, they must enforce it, and ensure that records are kept.

Electricity

While electricity is a vital part of our life and work in the twenty-first century, no one should be in any doubt that it can easily kill anyone who comes into direct contact with it. In theatre there is a large amount of electrical equipment that is constantly being moved and re-plugged, cables are used to provide temporary installa-

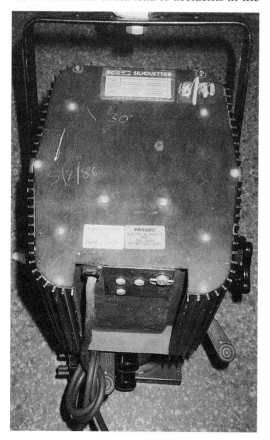

A PAT test label on a lantern.

tions, and these are all subject to damage from scenery being moved or people treading on them. Regular routine maintenance is therefore essential and, of course, has to be documented.

Portable appliance testing (PAT testing) is carried out regularly on all theatre electrical equipment, perhaps annually by a resident LX staff, but every time it goes out on hire by a hire company. The item will have an identifying label that states when it was last tested, and when the next test is due. Visiting amateur companies may be expected to supply PAT test records for any equipment they bring into a theatre (including performers' personal belongings such as hair dryers or radios).

Everyone working in theatre should, as a matter of course, inspect electrical equipment for any obvious defects before they plug it in or use it. They should also check that the PAT test label is not out of date. There should be a clear, published reporting system for any defects, and suspect equipment should not be used until it has been checked by a qualified electrician.

Ideally, all electrical outlets in a theatre will have up-to-date protection that detects any problem and trips out before any injury can be sustained (known as RCD protection). However, this is expensive and may not always be in place. Anyone working in an unfamiliar theatre should find out if this protection is available, and if it is not, should be even more careful than usual when using electrical equipment. The use of lower voltage equipment and tools, whenever possible, will also reduce the risk.

Trailing leads on stage are a particular hazard: they should be run in neatly and be taped down or covered with protective matting, and all staff and performers should be encouraged to report any that they believe to be a hazard, so that LX staff can make them safe.

Working at Heights

The danger of working at height, as illustrated in the photograph, is obvious because it is

An example of 'working at height', in this case an actor being flown. Photo: GSMD archives

unusual. However, the design of a theatre means that working at height is a regular part of the job for many theatre employees, and there is a danger that they become oblivious to the risk involved. They must be aware that one mistake could cost them their lives, and always take every necessary precaution. The correct use of equipment, whether it is specialized access equipment or safety equipment, must be observed at all times. It can be a great temptation, particularly when under pressure as an opening night approaches, to try and save time by cutting corners, taking a risk, or leaning out that little bit further from a ladder or catwalk. It is the production manager's responsibility to instil a culture of safe working at all times, and this should extend to rigorous checking of the equipment used for working at height during productions.

People working at heights should be aware that it is not just they who are in danger, but that dropping anything from a height can have severe consequences for anyone below. Having to wear your hard hat may seem to be a chore, particularly if it is hot and the overhead work is only going on for a few minutes, but production managers must ensure that hard hat policies are enforced, and should devise some sort of system, perhaps involving a flashing beacon, so that anyone entering the stage area knows when hard hats should be worn.

Lifting Regulations

As well as working at height, in the theatre industry heavy loads are suspended above the heads of performers, technicians and sometimes members of the audience. What is more, those loads are then moved, often in darkness and at speed. It is only because this is done in a rehearsed situation that we do not have to sound alarm bells or activate flashing lights before moving them.

It is particularly important that all of this activity – known as flying – is carried out safely and with the correct, certified equipment that is checked before it is used. Inexperienced staff should be supervised when using flying equipment.

Holes in the Ground

As if large amounts of electricity, and working and suspending things high in the air with reduced light levels were not enough, people in theatres also like to open holes in the stage to allow for things to appear and disappear, perhaps through trap doors.

There can be no doubt that falling through a trap door could be fatal, so as far as the risk rating matrix is concerned, its severity is *extreme*. Therefore in order to keep the risk rating at an acceptable level of *medium*, there have to be systems in place that mean that such a fall is *highly unlikely* to occur. This may be possible to achieve during performances, as the relevant section of the show can be planned and rehearsed so that no one is near the trap door when it is open. Regulating it during technical rehearsals, and even during the fit-up, however, is much more difficult. The production manager must ensure there are measures in place to guarantee everyone's safety when traps are open during these times. Probably the best way to do this is to make it one person's responsibility to guard the trap at all times when it is open and the relevant scene is not actually being rehearsed. It may be that the person at most risk is not any of the performers or crew, but the director, as they will be concentrating on other things and can easily be unaware of an unguarded open trap.

How this hazard is going to be addressed must form part of the production's risk assessment, and everyone must be aware of it.

The safety of orchestra pits, another regular feature of many productions, must also be addressed, particularly to make sure that members of the public cannot fall in. Again it may be during the setting up of the pit that most hazards are present.

EXAMPLE OF A CODE OF PRACTICE FOR USING HARD HATS

Once issued with them **everyone** working on stage **must** wear a **hard hat** during the following times:

• From the start of the **get out** to the **end of the fit up.**
• Whenever work is being carried out on the **fly floor.**
• Whenever work is being carried out on the **grid.**
• Whenever work is being carried out on the **tallescope.**
• Whenever **rigging** is being carried out on **bridges.**
• When ever the Hard Hat Lights are operating

Hard Hat Lights

These are flashing green beacons in the Prompt Corner and O.P. Corner. They will be switched on whenever Hard Hats are being used and no one should enter the stage area without wearing a Hard Hat when the beacons are operating.

Issue of Hats

Each permanent member of technical staff will be issued with their own HARD HAT. They will be asked to sign for receipt of the hat and that it is suitable for them. Casuals should collect hats from Stage Door or the stairwells on their way to the stage and return them there at the end of the call. The colour coding is BLUE for LX, RED for STAGE MANAGEMENT, YELLOW for STAGE casuals, WHITE for LX casuals.

Procedure

• Anyone going to the **fly floor** or **grid** will announce that they are doing so.
• Anyone rigging on **foh bridges** will announce that they are about to do so
• The **person climbing** the **tallescope** will announce that they are about to use the tallescope
• The **person in charge** on stage will ensure that **everyone** puts on their hat and that the Hard Hat Lights are put on. (The person in charge is the Production Manager, Chief LX, or senior member of department)

Work must not commence on the flyfloor, grid or bridges and the tallescope must not be climbed until everyone has their Hard Hat on
    Once work on the fly floors, grid, bridges or tallescope has finished this should be announced to the person in charge. They will, if appropriate, announce that hard hats can be removed and turn off the Hard Hat Lights.

Storage of Hats

When not in use hats should be kept on the hooks in the stairwells to the Stage or in your own department

---

Fire

In order to be granted their licence, theatres must be well equipped for identifying and dealing with an outbreak of fire. This is just as well, because in a large number of productions there is a requirement to set fire to something flammable in close proximity to large numbers of members of the public. Some productions require this as part of the plot, for example the burning of crucial manuscripts. Others need it to create period authenticity, or to add effect, for example candles or flaming torches. Many actors and directors seem to feel that their characters must smoke a cigarette at crucial parts of the play. Part of the licensing inspection will therefore require a 'flame plot', listing what naked flame is used and when, for how long, where and by whom, together with what safety measures are in place.

Production managers should also be aware of the implications of using theatrical smoke on stage. In order to create the right effect, it may be necessary to de-activate the smoke detection in the stage area. This is unlikely to be a problem while there are cast, crew and audience in the theatre, as the outbreak of a real fire would be quickly recognized; but it must be ensured that there are fail-safe systems in place for switching detection back on as soon as possible. Apart from not wanting the theatre to burn down, it will probably be found that any insurance is invalid if automatic detection is not in place.

Apart from when it is needed on stage as part of the action, smoking should only be allowed in a few designated parts of the building.

Noise

Although it may be a factor for short periods of time in productions, and will therefore feature in the production risk assessment, noise is more likely to be a major consideration in the building or task risk assessment. Noise is measured cumulatively, and therefore staff spending most of their working lives in an environment surrounded by noisy machinery are much more at risk that those exposed to short periods of very loud noise during a production.

Specialist equipment or companies may need to be employed to measure the noise levels and suggest action to be taken. If it is not practicable to eliminate the risk by removing the machinery altogether, it may be possible to make the workshop a safer place by replacing or re-siting machinery, having better maintenance (blunt blades make more noise than sharp ones), or adding dampening or acoustic panels. If this does not reduce noise levels suffi-

ciently, ear protection may need to be considered. There are two 'action levels' with regard to this: first at a noise level of 85dB(A), when the employer must provide ear protection; secondly at 90 dB(A), when the employer must ensure that ear protection is worn.

The recommended or compulsory wearing of ear protection must be included in the code of practice for each machine, and depending on the design of the space, applies not only to those using the machinery, but also to others working in, or visiting the department.

Hazardous Substances

In a theatre environment, hazardous substances exist in most backstage departments. Paintshops and props workshops will have them in the form of glues, resins and solvent-based paints, and the hazards of spraying should be seriously considered. In scenic workshops, airborne dust and welding fumes are classed as hazardous substances. Dyes, cleaning solutions and polishes will need assessing in wardrobe, while LX and sound departments should be aware of the hazards of fumes from soldering. Hazardous substances are less likely to appear in a production risk assessment except, perhaps, for theatrical smoke or dry ice.

Whether hazardous or not, all products purchased should have information regarding their composition and possible risks displayed on their packaging. In addition, data sheets must be supplied by the manufacturers on request.

In the UK, the legislation that deals with this is known as COSHH (Control of Substances Hazardous to Health). An assessment needs to be undertaken that:

- lists all substances used in the theatre;
- identifies what hazards they may present;
- finds out who could be exposed, and how;
- quantifies the exposure by measuring level, length and frequency of exposure;
- decides if there is a risk involved;

- decides what measures are needed;
- records the assessment together with a review date.

As with all health and safety issues, it is best to remove the risk if possible by ceasing to use the substance. Water-based varnishes and paints are now available that have features previously only available from solvent-based products; different types of glue may also be used.

If an alternative product or method cannot be found, steps must be taken to reduce employees' exposure, either by installing specialist fume and dust extraction, or by specialist paint booths.

The final resort is the use of masks and respirators, but this is the least satisfactory solution.

Manual Handling

More than a quarter of all work-related injuries reported each year can be directly attributed to manual handling; that is, the moving of objects by hand or bodily force. Theatre tends to be a very manual industry, with many one-off tasks that it is difficult to legislate for; but there are a number of areas where manual handling problems have or could be reduced.

The designers of new or refurbished theatre buildings should have taken manual handling into account by installing goods lifts to all levels, having lorry-back height access to stage and workshops, and by installing power flying. In existing buildings, it is possible to go some distance towards reducing the need to lift heavy objects by installing winches or cranes, by using palletizers or forklift trucks, by putting wheels on all boxes and crates, and by considering how storage spaces are used.

However, there are still certain areas in the work of most departments where manual handling cannot be completely avoided. Here a manual handling assessment, consideration of the redesign of tasks, work spaces and equipment, and staff training all have to be undertaken. Specialist training in awareness and lifting techniques is the first step for all theatre employees. Staff particularly need to forget the macho attitude to moving heavy objects, to assess the task before they start it, work in teams and ask for help where necessary.

Working Hours

Legislation is now starting to be enforced that stipulates the number of hours that can be worked without a rest period, and dictates the minimum length of breaks, and this is affecting the way in which theatres can operate.

The production manager needs to become fully aware of the terms of the legislation, and discuss it with their management and staff to see how it affects the scheduling of work. Staff can opt out from the legislation, but should not be put under any pressure to do so. As with all health and safety matters, records need to be kept in case of inspection or query.

CONCLUSION

Health and safety is a huge responsibility for production managers, and legislation has greatly increased their workload over recent years. Every production manager wants to work safely and not put their staff at risk, but it is the recording of all assessments, factors, occurrences and decisions that makes it such a daunting task.

Production managers can also find themselves caught between managements who want to keep expenditure on staff to a minimum and turn shows round as quickly as possible, and some staff who are unwilling to embrace health and safety fully, as they feel they have worked safely for years and do not understand the need for codes of practice. The aim must be to introduce a culture of working safely at all times, while also proving that you are doing so by carrying out and recording all the required assessments and checks.

6   REHEARSING THE SHOW

In this chapter and the next we will look at the parallel processes of rehearsing a production in the rehearsal room and preparing the physical requirements of the show. Although separate, it is important that these two activities are linked and that there is continuous, complete and accurate communication between the rehearsal room and those making, acquiring and adapting items for the production.

Professional productions rehearse for a limited, concentrated period of time, which demands almost total commitment to the production being rehearsed. Rehearsals for amateur productions will take place over a longer, less intensive period in the evenings and at weekends, but still need to be organized, staffed and monitored in the same way. A production manager's involvement with rehearsals on a day-to-day basis is limited, but they need to know what should be happening and be sure that they have the staff in place to ensure that it does happen. Anything not dealt with properly in rehearsals, or information not passed back to those realizing the production, can cause expensive, time-consuming delays when the show moves into the theatre. The DSM is the most important member of staff in this process, and their responsibilities are described in detail, together with everything that needs to be organized for rehearsals to run smoothly.

THE FIRST DAY'S REHEARSAL

At the very start of rehearsals, those involved in the two processes of rehearsing and realizing the production will meet together. The first day of rehearsals usually begins with a **meet and greet** at which the creative team, production team, performers and administration staff are all present. This is partly, but not entirely, a social event, and if the company is building-based, usually takes place in the theatre building rather than the rehearsal room. The performers may possibly be strangers to the area, may not yet have met each other, and will not know all of the production or administration staff. Refreshments should be available, there should be a brief welcome by, ideally, the artistic director or chief executive, and everyone should be introduced or should introduce themselves. Any key personnel not present should also be mentioned.

Administration departments will want to take advantage of all the company being in one place to get any information they need. The finance department will want to check information needed for paying salaries; publicity will want information for the programme and may want to talk about any marketing initiatives in which the company will be involved. (The 'company' is the global name for all the actors and dancers in a production. A rehearsal involving all the cast is therefore known as a 'company call'.)

Stage management will want to acquire or check performers' contact details, especially the address where they can be contacted during the rehearsal and performance period. A good stage management team will also have produced a fact sheet or welcome booklet telling the company everything they need to know about the theatre and the town. Amateur performers will be local to the town in which they are rehearsing but may still appreciate having rehearsal schedules, information about the company, and the venue in which they will be performing.

After this type of business has been concluded, there will usually be a design presentation. The director will talk about the concept of the production, and the set designer will describe and present the set model to the company, who will also be shown the costume designs. This may also be the first opportunity for the wardrobe department to measure the actors, and should be discussed in advance when planning the day.

The meet and greet and design presentation will probably have taken the whole morning, particularly if a tour of the building is included, so it will be after lunch that the read-through takes place. At this the company, director and DSM sit round a table in the rehearsal room with their copy of the script and read the play out loud. The production manager, the stage management team, the designers and key staff (notably wardrobe) should stay for this read-through, as there may be queries about technical moments that can be answered. Also, particularly if it is a new piece, it is fascinating to hear a company read a play for the first time. If it is a musical, the company will not yet have learned any of the songs, but the musical director may play some of them on the piano.

Also as part of the read-through, the director will probably announce any cuts to the script and, if the piece does not break down into suitably sized scenes, may decide on the blocks into which the show will be split for rehearsals.

A meet and greet in progress. Photo: Martin Hazlewood

Cuts and Copyright

Both professional and amateur companies must obtain permission to perform the piece before announcing it, starting rehearsals or booking a theatre. As well as gaining permission from the copyright owner to perform a piece, permission may have to be sought to make cuts to the text. The director needs to be sure that this is permitted under the terms of the licence. Some shows cannot be cut or changed in any way, and copyright remains in force until seventy years after the author's death.

After the read-through, rehearsals proper can start. As already described (*see* Chapter 3), the DSM will be at every rehearsal; the stage manager may also stay at this point, but everyone else will leave. The director may want to start rehearsing the play, or they may want to

discuss the text and the characters, or do some improvisation. If the decision is to do text analysis or discussion, the company (and the DSM) will remain sitting round the table – this can continue for several days, especially if the text is difficult, such as Shakespeare. Otherwise stage management will clear away the table and chairs to reveal the mark-up.

The mark-up:

- is a full-scale representation of the set on the rehearsal room floor.
- is done using PVC tape, a different colour for each scene.
- must include the centre-line of the stage.
- has marks for furniture added during the rehearsal period – these are then transferred back to the theatre for the start of the focusing session.
- should include the sightlines from the extreme seats in the theatre.
- may need to be reduced if the rehearsal room is smaller than the stage – in this case,

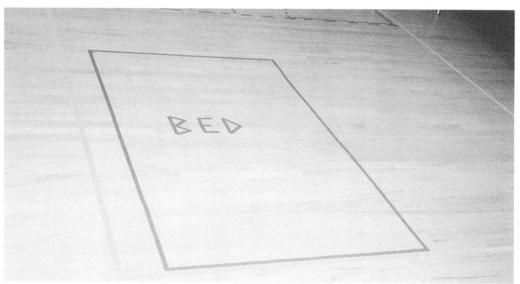

Detail of a mark-up in a rehearsal room. Photo: Hannah Dickinson

a transparent copy of a scale drawing of the rehearsal room can be overlaid on the ground plan to see how the mark-up can best fit.

- should be discussed with the director in advance to agree their location relative to any natural light and doors.
- may need to be on carpet or a floor cloth if rehearsals are going to move rooms frequently.
- is useful for the production manager to look at, as it gives an idea of how big the set will be at full size.

There may be a conflict of interests at this point, which is a good example of the sort of problems production management need to anticipate and deal with. The director may want the model of the set to remain in the rehearsal room while the actors start to work on the play, but it is likely also to be needed by the paintshop if they have started work on the production. The production manager may have to negotiate with both parties – the director may be satisfied with a good photograph of the model plus a groundplan (which should be displayed in the rehearsal room anyway), and the paintshop may need only a piece of the model, not all of it.

For a musical or pantomime there may be up to three rehearsals taking place at the same time in three separate spaces. The musical director may be teaching some of the company a musical number, the director rehearsing one of the scenes, while the choreographer may be setting another number. This needs to have been allowed for at the planning stage. Stage management need to have decided how they are going to staff these rehearsals, and to ascertain whether additional pianos, accompanists or recordings of the music are required.

Communication from Rehearsals

Every director will work in a different way, and although the production manager will not be actively involved in rehearsals, it is important to know how the director works, and when they intend to block the play, as this will affect the flow of information from rehearsals.

If the director works slowly through the play agreeing every piece of blocking and discussing motivation and character, there will be a steady stream of information and requests. If they block the play quickly, there will be a lot of information and requests at the beginning, and then more detail later. If they use a lot of improvisation as a way into each character and use the actual text later, there may be no information to start with, and then a flood. This is the most difficult method of working to deal with, and the production manager and their stage management team need to make it clear to this director that there is certain information that departments need in order to do their work. All directors need to

Blocking

The moves that actors make in a production, the process of deciding what the moves should be, and the recording of them, are all known as blocking. The DSM will write in the prompt script every move that each actor makes, and when they make it, and they will indicate the exact word on which this happens. This is so that, when the scene is revisited in the rehearsal room, the DSM can remind the actors and the director of the agreed moves.

Blocking is always done in pencil, as it is subject to frequent changes. It is also used for reference during lighting sessions, and for rehearsing understudies or cast replacements in long-running professional productions.

be informed of the cut-off date for decisions from the rehearsal room, after which departments may not be able to take changes or additions on board.

Whatever the rehearsal method used, the ever-present and alert DSM will note everything that happens and will communicate all decisions, changes, questions and requests to the production manager and all technical departments by producing daily rehearsal notes or reports.

The DSM should also take notice of any informal conversations that take place in and around the rehearsal room when people are not actually rehearsing. The leading man and director may be discussing last night's football match or the quality of the coffee, but equally they may be deciding on a major change to a prop or costume, which the relevant department needs to know about.

For a production manager, rehearsal reports are the most important piece of paperwork coming from the rehearsal room. They should be numbered consecutively and dated, and should have a section for each department, including a general section and one for the designer. Each point will have a reference number, and the report will be distributed to each department, even if there is apparently nothing on the report specific to them.

Requirements for any area of the production that are discussed in rehearsals should go on that day's report if, in the DSM's opinion:

• it affects any department other than stage management;
• it is a new item;
• it is a change to an item already known about, or referred to on a previous note (give the reference);
• it is a change in use of something;
• it means altering something from stock;

• it means that something has been cut;
• there are budgetary implications (good or bad);
• there are health and safety or fire implications;
• the designer or lighting designer might need to know or give an answer;
• either the director or designer (or both) will disagree with, or not understand, the implications of a decision;
• it needs further discussion or clarification.

Rehearsal reports are not easy to write, and the production manager will want to encourage their team to produce reports that are unambiguous to everyone's interpretation of them; use the agreed name for the item or scene; give all the information; give the current situation; and that consider all the implications. As they are distributed every day, they can also be used as a means of communicating information that needs to be available to everyone working on the production, for example something about the set that has been changed during the build period.

It is a good idea for the production manager to visit rehearsals every so often, even just for a few minutes, and get a flavour of how things are going there. It is surprising how often a technical issue comes up in a rehearsal while the production manager is there. This can save a lot of time later on. They should also make a point of visiting the stage management office at the end of the day's rehearsal, where the DSM will be briefing the rest of the team on what has happened and what is planned for the next day. The production manager may be able to answer a lot of their questions, and will become aware at an early stage of items that may develop into problems. They can also help to advise on what should go on to rehearsal notes, and how they should be worded.

GOING INTO SHADOWS	Rehearsal Note 4

Date: Thursday 3rd May 2001   Director: Stephen Medcalf
Venue: Rehearsal Room B   D.S.M: Julia Mathes

General:
1. A reminder that there will be a progress meeting on Monday (7th) at 9.30am in the Meeting Room
2. Is it possible for the chorus to enter via the auditorium doors and walk down the aisles for Act 1, scene 2? This is to cover the scene change between scenes 1 and 2.

Stage Management:
1. Two stacks of towels are required on the cleaner's trolley in act 1, scene 2.
2. The bank notes will need to be £50 notes. There needs to be £800 worth.
3. The lighter in act 1, scene 10 needs to be practical.
4. New prop. A British Museum catalogue is required for act 1, scene 4, and should be dated 1985.
5. The suitcases will need to be strong enough to be sat on by the chorus members.
6. The Financial Times will not be rolled up any more. They will now be preset folded on the floor behind the counter. The Sun will still be rolled up.
7. The glass of milk in act 3, scene 2 has been cut.

Wardrobe:
1. Are the coats in act 1, scene 12 all the same colour?
2. A rehearsal cardigan is required for Patrick (Doug Bowen).
3. Patrick's (Doug Bowen) cardigan will need a pocket to hold a packet of cigarettes

Props:
1. The vase in the box (act 1, scene 2) should have a handle on it.

Workshop:
1. In act 1, scene 4, the Bartender (Mr Franck Lopez) will walk along the counter and jump off it.

Sound:
1. The string quartet in act 1, scene 4 will need to be amplified.

Production Management
1. The implications of Workshop note 1 are to be included in the production risk assessment.

Electrics
1. See general note
2. The director would like them to sing the first part from the auditorium, therefore they will need to be lit.

There are no notes for paintshop
Thank you,

Kate John
Stage Manager

Distribution: Director, Designer, Lighting Designer, Production Management, Technical Management, SM, DSM, ASMs, Wardrobe, Props, Paintshop, Workshop, LX, Sound

An example of a rehearsal note.

THE BOOK

The DSM is responsible for the book, also known as the prompt script or prompt copy. This starts off as a copy of the script with each page pasted onto a blank sheet of paper in an A4 lever arch file. The script is generally on the right, with a blank page on the left. This blank page is used to record three pieces of information: the cues, the blocking, and the backstage and front-of-house calls. In the file there should eventually be a copy of every piece of paperwork produced by stage management to do with the show, and relevant information from all other production departments.

Before rehearsals start, especially if it is a musical, the DSM will also obtain the sheet music of any music to be performed during the show. These will be added to the script in the prompt copy in such a way that the DSM can read from the end of a piece of dialogue into the music and back to dialogue at the end of

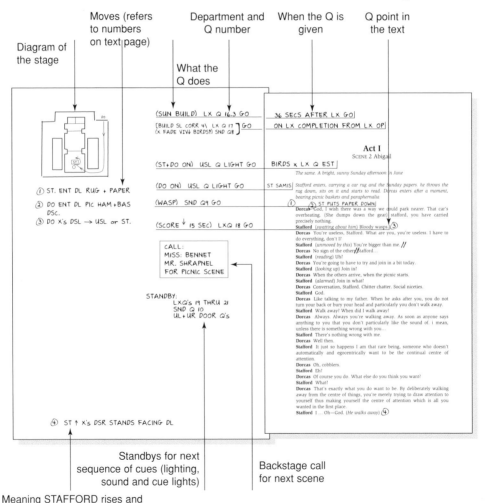

A page from a prompt copy.

the music. As decisions are made about these during rehearsals, they will also insert the music for pieces played at the start of the play, in scene changes and at the end of the piece. This is so that later on they can insert any cues that need to be given during musical passages.

There are several ways of laying out prompt copies, but the stage manager will be aware that in an emergency, other members of the department may be required to run the show using the prompt copy. They may therefore wish to standardize the way their team lay out their prompt copies. It is also not unknown for the production manager to have to run the show in an extreme emergency, so they will want to be sure they know how the book is being laid out. They will also want to be sure that all the information that might be needed is in the book, so that there are no hold-ups at the technical rehearsal.

At this point in the process a major part of the DSM's work is the blocking. If there are obvious technical cues – for instance a blackout at the end of the scene, or a clap of thunder – the DSM may also start to pencil these in. The DSM may be required to undertake cues in the rehearsal room that will later be done by others. These could include doorbells or knocks, furniture and props changes, or reading in voice-overs. These will all be written in the book, and will also be used as the basis for running plots for ASMs and crew. Sound effects would also be mentioned on rehearsal notes to inform or remind the sound designer.

Usually once a director has worked right through a play (which can take several days or longer), they will go back to the beginning and begin to put sections and scenes together. It is here that the DSM's skills in notating blocking and prompting are paramount. It is unlikely that the actors or the director will remember all the moves they agreed, and so they will ask the DSM for clarification of what these were. From notes in the prompt copy the DSM should be able to tell them.

The DSM will also put all cuts and changes to the text into the book. Once the actors start to learn their lines and work without a script in their hand (known as being 'off the book') they will rely on the DSM to prompt them if they forget their lines. Good prompting is an important skill for stage management to acquire. It does not come easily to many people, and part of the rapport that a good DSM builds up with each performer is knowing when they need prompting. The correct thing for an actor to say is 'line', though very often, in the heat of the moment, this is not the word they use!

In professional theatre, prompts are not given in performance, and actors are expected to get themselves back on track if they forget their lines. In amateur theatre, a separate person from the DSM is often used to prompt performers, and it is important that this person is not brought in at the last minute but attends as many rehearsals as possible so that they get to know the piece and the performers and do not prompt when an actor is pausing for dramatic effect.

OTHER REHEARSAL ISSUES

The DSM is also responsible for producing rehearsal calls. It is unlikely that every performer is in every scene, and the director will decide which scene will be rehearsed and when. Company members will just be called for the scenes or blocks they are in. Stage management use an availability chart that they produce before rehearsals start, to determine who is in each scene, and then produce a call sheet for each day. The production manager should get a copy. The call sheet will also include calls for costume fittings, wardrobe shopping, publicity and so on, which the relevant departments will have requested via the stage manager.

Hopefully the director will plan rehearsals in advance and give the company plenty of

GOING INTO SHADOWS		**Rehearsal Call Friday 11th May 2001**	
	Rehearsal Room B		Wardrobe
10.00am	Act 2, scene 4 Miss Natasha Jouhl Miss Katarina Jovanovic	10.00	Miss Lise Christensen
11.00am	to join: Miss Camilla Roberts Mr David Clegg Mr Haydn Jones	11.00 11.30	Miss Alenka Ponjavic Miss Sarah Redgwick
12.00	**Full chorus to join**	12.00	Mr Doug Bowen
1.00pm	Lunch	1.00	Wardrobe fittings end
2.00pm	Act 3, scene 3 Miss Lise Christensen Miss Alenka Ponjavic Miss Sarah Redgwick		
3.30pm	to join Mr Doug Bowen Mr Breffni Horgan Mr Andy Rees		
5.00pm	Tea		
6.00pm	Act 3, scene 4 Miss Sarah Redgwick Mr Barry Martin		
8.30pm	**Call ends**		

Thank you,

Kate John
Stage Manager

Distribution: Director, Designer, Conductor, Production Management, SM, DSM, ASMs, SM Office, Wardrobe Supervisor, Wardrobe Office, Rehearsal Room Notice Board, Stage Door

An example of a rehearsal call sheet with wardrobe calls.

notice as to when they will be needed. Not all directors are good at this, however, and there are union rules about when the next day's call must be published. If it is very late this makes extra work for stage management, as they will have to phone each member of the company to inform them what their call is. Very occasionally the production manager may have to step in if the director is infringing rules about calls. They will also want to make sure that

OPPOSITE: An example of a props list.

GOING INTO SHADOWS PROPS LIST (As Agreed at the Production Meeting)

SCENE	ITEM	SOURCE	BUDGET	NOTES	FOUND	COLLECTED	APPROVED
Scene 1 **The Hotel Room**	Cleaner's trolley	Borrow (hotel)		Must be strong enough to be sat on exact items to be confirmed			
	Dressing for trolley	Hire	£50.00	Chrome legs (see model)			
	Circular glass topped table	Buy	£25.00	Will need plug changing by LX			
	Light	Buy	£10.00	Wooden			
	Fruit bowl	Buy	£10.00	3 apples, 2 oranges. 1 'exotic' fruit			
	Fruit						
Scene 4 **The Wine Bar**	4 × chairs	Find		Matching wooden seats, thin chrome legs			
	32 × Financial Times	Donation		FT numbers in contact book			
	32 × The Sun	Donation		Headline needs to be non-descript			
	32 × bottles of lager	Donation		Budweiser (or Becks). Open but not drunk			
	Metal tray	Stock		Round chrome to take Perrier and glasses	✓	In SM store	
	2 × small bottles of Perrier	Stock			✓	In SM store	
	2 × glass tumblers	Stock			✓	In SM store	
	2 × cappucino cups	Stock			✓	In SM store	
Scene 6 **Silk Shop**	3 × lengths of silk	Buy (Brick Lane)	£125.00	1 @ 15m. 2 @ 5m. Take designer	✓	In wardrobe	
	6 × cloth tape measures	Wardrobe					
	6 × name plates	SM make		See designer for reference			
Scene 8 **The Bedsit**	Armchair	Junk shop	see sofa	To match sofa (scene 10) Props to re-cover			
	Throw	Buy	£10.00	Dark blue. Comes off for scene 10			
	70s light fitting	LX stock		Practical. Flys in	✓	LX store	
	Vodka bottle	Stock		Should be half full	✓	In SM store	
	Glass tumbler	Stock			✓	In SM store	
Scene 10 **Parent's House**	Two seater sofa	Junkshop	£100.00	To match armchair (scene 8) Props store-cover			
	Coffee table	Junkshop	£10.00	Cheap and tasteless			
	Kettle & flex	Stock		Set under sink. Dressing only			
	Assorted cleaning materials	Stock					
	Tray	Stock		Rectangular wooden			
	Teaset	Find		4 cups and saucers, sugar bowl, milk jug			
	4 teaspoons	Stock		Stainless steel			
	Tea caddy and loose tea	Buy sundries					

actors' overtime is being kept to a minimum (the DSM will keep time sheets for all the company), and that stage management are getting proper breaks and not incurring too much overtime. However, because of the vital role a DSM has in the process, it is often not possible for them to avoid overtime completely.

Stage management are also responsible for co-ordinating actors' calls to be fitted in or go shopping for their costume. These are known as 'wardrobe calls' and will be requested by the wardrobe supervisor, usually with a specific time or times in mind. Stage management and particularly the DSM need to negotiate actors' availability for these with the director.

Calls for Fittings

It is often the view of wardrobe departments, unfortunately, that stage management do not negotiate hard enough with the director for fittings to happen at the requested time. They need to bear in mind the life of the wardrobe department, the fact that outside makers may be involved, or that visits to shops may be needed. They should also think about how long it will take to get from the rehearsal room, and make sure the actors leave on time. Occasionally production management may have to step in and persuade the director that if they want their actors to have costumes, they must be released from rehearsals for fittings.

Sometimes a professional performer may be rehearsing one production during the day and performing another, perhaps at a different theatre, at night. They may also have commitments to TV or film work that will take them out of rehearsals. These should have been agreed with the director at contract stage. Amateur performers, where there is a long rehearsal period, may also have some rehearsals that they cannot attend. On both professional and amateur productions, stage management should be informed of these as early as possible, and should keep a record of these commitments – known as being not available or N/A – which they can refer to when working out calls with the director.

Stage management will have produced a provisional props list from their first reading of the play, and will have amended this with information from the first production meeting and their meeting with the director and designer. They will have produced a revised props list, a copy of which should always be in rehearsals and which should be further amended as things change (*see* page 119).

A rehearsal version of every prop and piece of furniture in the show should be available from day one: this is where a good props store can be a great help. There may have to be some budget available for making or hiring rehearsal versions of pieces of the set. This particularly applies if there are elements that the actors have to work with that it would take too much time or be too dangerous for them to encounter for the first time they got on stage. Raised levels, staircases and raked floors are such items, and it is a good idea to have some free-standing rehearsal doors available.

The DSM should also have a copy of every department's costing for the show so that, if it comes up during rehearsals, they know what is being produced.

As soon as possible – and, like production budgets, rehearsal time is never enough – scenes will start to be run. Stage management will advise those interested, especially lighting and sound designers, so that they can attend. The ASM may also need to be in rehearsals at this point to assist with scene changes and to learn their involvement in the show.

*OPPOSITE: **An example of a running plot.***

THIS PRODUCTION
Running Plot (Version 2)

Pre show	Shout check	(ASMs)	
	Check cans and Q lights	(DSM and sound operator)	
	Fire drill	(All SM and LX operator)	
	Set remaining furniture	(ASMs)	
Beginners	Stage right	Miss Allam, Miss Boyd, Mr Brooksbank, Mr Saunders	
	Stage left	Mr Robertson, Mr Thornton	
On clearance	Send on Miss Boyd and Mr Thornton		ASMs

ACT 1 SCENE 1 (The Hospital) Pages 1 to 5

p5	End of scene 1		
	Strike bed		Crew
	Fly Q1	Wall Out (Bar 16)	Flys
	f/o	Drape in (Bar 10)	Flys
	Quick change	Miss Boyd (SR quick change room)	Wardrobe and Wigs

ACT 1 SCENE 2 (The Artist's Studio) pages 5 to 23

p7	Page door for Mr Robertson and Mr Thornton		SR ASM
p9	Light candle and hand to Miss Allam		SL ASM
p11	Receive candle from Miss Allam and extinguish		SL ASM
p20	After Mr Robertson's exit, preset all furniture for scene 3 by SR door		ASMs
	(table with 4 chairs on it, standard lamp, trolley, armchair)		
p23	End of scene 2		
	Fly Q2	Drape out (Bar 10)	Flys
	Set table and 4 chairs (yellow marks)		ASMs
	Exit SL with 4 cushions (SR ASM) and tray of glasses (SL ASM)		
	Set standard lamp (SR ASM) and trolley (SL ASM)		
	Follow SR ASM on (2nd entrance) and set armchair (yellow marks)		Crew

ACT 1 SCENE 3 (The Parent's House) pages 23 to 40

	no Stage Management Qs during this scene		
	prepare food for Act 2 Scene 1		ASMs
p40	End of Act 1 Scene 3		
	Page Miss Allam and Mr Thornton off in Blackout		SR ASM

Clear line of safety curtain, give clearance to prompt corner, watch safety curtain in   ASMs

Interval Change

	Strike all furniture except table and 4 chairs	ASMs
	Collect Miss Boyd's blue dress from settee	Wardrobe
	Set meal (see Act 2 setting list)	ASMs

Provided the director has no objections, the production manager should feel free to attend any rehearsal that is dealing with a scene involving specific technical moments they need to know more about. They should know from the rehearsal call sheet when this will be happening, and should also make a point of dropping into rehearsals from time to time, perhaps when passing the rehearsal room for another reason.

Running Plots

Working from information they noted at the first production meeting and subsequent meetings with production and technical management, the DSM will have a draft running plot, detailing the main scene changes, early on in rehearsals. Working with the stage manager, they will add to and amend these as rehearsals progress, putting in more and more detail, including who is responsible for each item, where they move to and from, how long there is between changes, and any resetting that needs to happen. The completed plot should detail what happens to every piece of scenery, furniture and major prop during the running of the show. Plots will be issued to those who need them before the final run-through.

Setting Lists

The position where everything starts at the top of the show is detailed in a separate document known as the 'setting list'. These:

- ensure that everything is ready and working for each performance, and can be found in exactly the same place every time.
- should include all props, furniture and dressing, both onstage and offstage, in the position where they are at the start of the show.
- should be based on a diagram (not to scale) of the stage, set and fixed items; sub-drawings of individual settings will probably also be needed.
- should work logically round the stage and tell stage management everything they need to know about the setting of each item.

- should include all details of how items need to be set, and any checks that need to be made.
- should include everything needed for the show backstage – for example, chairs for people to sit on, headsets, brooms, bins, tools for doing interval changes.
- should also include a list of everything that needs checking for working, such as motors, traps, doors and any movable scenery; or for damage, such as scuffs and dents; and any masking that specifically needs checking.
- will need revising once the production gets on stage.
- must be sensitive to how the performers want things setting.
- should include a separate sheet of 'personal' props that are to be found in the dressing rooms or in items of costume.
- should be 'shout-checked', as should the pre-set and the interval pre-set on the running plot. This involves one member of the team reading out each item on the list, and another member confirming that it is in place.
- should be in enough detail that even someone who is not familiar with the production could set it up in an emergency.

THE FINAL RUN-THROUGH

Just as everyone got together at the beginning of the rehearsal process, so they do at the end. The final run-through is the big moment before the show moves into the theatre. It takes place in the rehearsal room, but is as near a performance of the piece as is possible in that situation. It should be attended by all the creative team, the production manager, all stage management, the wardrobe supervisor, the technical manager, the chief LX and, ideally, all those working on the show – the LX and sound operators, followspot operators, crew and dressers.

OPPOSITE: *An example of a setting list.*

THIS PRODUCTION
Setting List (version 2)

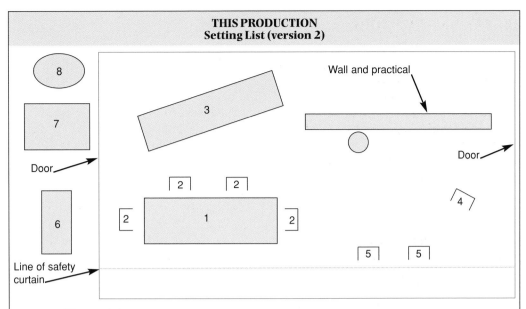

Onstage (blue marks)

    Table DSR (1)
    4 chairs round table (2)
    Hipflask and waitscoat on SR chair
    Ladder USR fully opened (3)
    Carver chair DSL (4)
    Wall flown in
    Check practical is plugged up
    2 chairs set upstage of safety curtain, ready to be set after fire drill (5)

Offstage
Stage Right Props Table (6)
    4 Comic Relief stickers
    Kate's handbag. In it: cigarettes (full pack)
                      lighter (check for working)
                        lipstick
    Bottle of champagne
    Bottle white wine (half full)
    Silver tray (square). On it: white cloth
                        4 glasses, half full of white wine

Under table
    Dustpan and brush
    Spanner and 4 bolts and length of sash for interval change

Behind set SR
    Porter's trolley (7). On it – top shelf:
                      Water jug
                      2 plastic cups
                      Roll of bin bags
                      bottom shelf
                      6 white towels
    Wheelchair with pink blanket folded on it (8)

It is the opportunity for production staff to see the piece without being concerned about operating their part of the show. The production manager, set and costume designers and HODs can see what has emerged from the rehearsal process, and can check that everything they have done and are planning to do at the fit-up is still appropriate. For lighting and sound designers it is a final chance to check cue positions, where actors are on stage, and timings of sections or scenes. Stage management will already be fairly familiar with the show, but as well as helping with the running of the rehearsal, it is their opportunity to rehearse props and furniture changes with all the team there. They should also get timings on scenes and acts, and should check that their paperwork is up to date, particularly setting and running lists.

The final run-through can be quite daunting for both director and performers. Their work from the whole rehearsal period is on semi-public show for the first time, and due to the pressure of time, it may be the first opportunity they have had to run the show right through without stopping. It is important for the company to realize that everyone there is part of the same team, and that staff are looking at the show from their own perspective and are not judging the quality of performances. Having said that, it is useful for the company, the director and the DSM if those who are watching a run actually react as an audience might do, as this will affect the timing of lines and cues. This includes laughing where appropriate, applauding at the end of musical numbers, joining in if there is audience participation, and applauding the company at the end of the show.

The production manager should make sure that they sit near the director and DSM so that they can ask questions about what is happening if necessary. Because there is unlikely to be a full set, or actual furniture or costumes in the rehearsal room, there will be certain actions that may need explaining. As with all those attending the run-through, the production manager should have all relevant paperwork including the script with him, and should be able to take notes as required.

After the run-through the director will want to have a notes session with the company. The production manager should try and have a few minutes with the director and the designers to discuss any queries or areas of concern that need sorting out before the fit-up, which is the next important moment in the production.

7 PREPARING THE SHOW

Production departments may have started their work on a show before the first rehearsal. Everyone will have their own responsibilities and work to do, though much of it will involve close liaison with other departments and staff. The production manager's job during the building of a show is mainly to facilitate the work of the production departments. As well as keeping an overview on everyone's work and being involved with any problems or conflicts, the production manager's work at this stage falls into five categories:

* risk assessments (*see* Chapter 5);
* finance;
* scheduling;
* preparing for production week;
* problem solving.

If the production manager is with a producing theatre or production company there will also be other shows at different stages of production, plus ongoing staffing and maintenance issues to deal with. With an amateur company that does not build its own scenery or make props or costumes, it may be mainly a question of arranging suitable hires; but the above five areas of work will still need to be addressed.

FINANCE

Many of the production manager's financial concerns will be to do with the purchasing or ordering of materials, and having systems in place to allow this to happen quickly and easily. There are five ways in which items can be bought, and the production manager will need to have set these up, or to know how they work:

* by order form and invoice;
* by pro forma invoice;
* by cash;
* by credit card;
* from stock.

So there is no delay in the purchasing process, and as long as the finance manager agrees, HODs can generally be allowed to make expenditure on the show up to the amount on their costing without referring to production management, provided they keep records. If, however, it is found that they are overspending or not keeping records, these privileges can be removed.

Order Form and Invoice
This is the best method of purchasing goods, as they will be despatched immediately and can be paid for later. An account facility needs to be set up in advance with each company, who will expect the theatre to use them regularly. Because of time scales and the huge variety and speciality of goods needed for different productions, this may not always be practical. An agreement will be needed as to who is to have a supply of blank order forms, and who is to be allowed to sign them.

Everyone's Work During the Preparation of a Production

Director	In rehearsals; Attending more and more meetings and discussions, especially with the lighting and sound designers; Looking at finished items with the designer and production manager.
Designer	In close contact with the director; More and more in evidence; Visiting each department and approving work; Spending most of their time in wardrobe, in fittings or shopping; Checking with the production manager at the end of each visit.
Lighting director	Finalising the lighting plan; Attending rehearsals as appropriate; Producing Q list; setting provisional Q points with the DSM; Liaising with the chief LX about equipment.
Sound designer	Preparing music and effects; Playing these to the director; Getting sound into rehearsals as appropriate; Producing Q list; setting provisional Q points with the DSM.
Stage manager	Completing the acquisition of props; Setting dates for delivery or collection; Making the paperwork props (letters, documents etc.); Getting actual props into rehearsal; Putting details from the rehearsal room on to the groundplan; Acquiring a detailed knowledge of the show.
DSM	Attending all rehearsals and meetings; Keeping the 'book' up to date; Putting Qs and calls into the book; Producing setting lists and running plots; Day to day paperwork - rehearsal notes, calls, company timesheets.
ASM	Working with the stage manager on propping the show; Attending rehearsals; Acquiring a detailed knowledge of the show; Working with setting lists and running plot.
Technical manager	Finalizing groundplan and hanging plot; Making sure stock available for fit-up; Making sure hardware and tools available for fit-up; Calling casuals for fit-up; Acquiring detailed knowledge of running plot and scene changes.
Construction	On target with build and paint schedule; Making sure stock available for fit up; Making sure hardware and tools available for fit up; Using up to date groundplan.
Paintshop	On target with build and paint schedule (aware of any delays in workshop); Ensuring designer is happy with the work; Preparing for fit up, especially for painting the floor.
Props	On target with producing props; Ensuring designer is happy with the work; Getting finished items into rehearsals; Aware of involvement in the fit up; Liaising with stage management over props which they are having difficulty in finding and which may have to be made.
Wardrobe	Hires arranged; Makes on target; Stock fitted; Ensuring designer is happy with the work; Consumables ordered (tights, spirit gum, washing powder); Actual shoes being worn in rehearsal; Costume plot being developed into setting, running and quick change plot in conjunction with the DSM; Dressing room list with Stage Manager; Preparing for costume parade if there is to be one.
Electrics	Lighting plan delivered; Circuits allocated; Hires arranged; Practicals found, bought, made and tested; Gel ordered and cut; Media for any projection produced; All equipment prepared; Fit up schedule agreed; Casuals called; Q sheet available.
Sound	Design finalised; Equipment agreed; Material edited; Q list available; Operator in rehearsals?; Fit up schedule agreed; Cans, Q lights and video requirements and position known; Orchestra pit layout known.

Pro-Forma Invoice

This is similar to using order forms and invoices, but is used where the theatre does not have an account facility. It is sometimes less convenient in that the goods are not despatched until payment has been received, which can cause delays.

Cash

Because of the one-off nature of many of the purchases for productions, this is often the quickest method of payment. However, there are security issues to bear in mind (involving the cash itself and the staff carrying it), and more paperwork is involved than with most of the other methods of payment. It is vital that receipts are kept for all cash purchases made.

Departments will expect the production manager to be able to supply them with petty cash quickly, and systems need to be in place to be able to do this. HODs should give as much notice as possible if they are going to need large amounts of petty cash.

Credit Card

Use of a company credit card can be a very good way of buying goods quickly, from a distance, or over the Internet. It is worth considering arranging a company credit card for production management and for any HODs who need to make a lot of varied expenditure, for example wardrobe and stage management. Again, there are security and record-keeping issues to bear in mind.

Stock

For a theatre that regularly produces scenery, this can be a good method of having frequently used goods available immediately, and because items are bought in bulk, cheaper prices may apply. However, it does need the agreement of the finance department because of security and cash flow implications, and it requires accurate record-keeping from staff; it

Useful Stock

- plywood (bought a pallet at a time);
- sawn or planed timber (bought 1,000m/3,000ft at a time);
- box-section steel (bought 100 lengths at a time);
- canvas and other scenic fabrics (bought a bolt at a time);
- frequently used paints (e.g. black and white emulsion);
- replacement lamps for stage lighting equipment (bought in bulk annually);
- adhesives.

also makes the running expenditure figures more difficult to produce.

As the production manager is ultimately responsible for financial expenditure on productions, they will want to have their own accurate, up-to-date information about what expenditure is being made on the show. Although wanting to avoid duplication of work, they will expect HODs to keep their own records (these will probably be slightly more up to date than the production office version). The finance department will also have their own records (which will be slightly less up to date than the production office ones). Once the show has opened, these three sets of records will have to be cross-checked or reconciled.

Records should be broken down by department and based on initial costings, as agreed at the final production meeting. They should include a reference, such as the order number or petty cash sheet number for ease of cross-checking. By using a computerized spreadsheet (*see* page 129), the records can be quickly updated, and can also be used to feed information into other spreadsheets such as records for the whole financial year. The

	Order form and invoice	Pro forma invoice	Cash	Credit card	Stock
For	Goods dispatched immediatly and paid for later	Allows purchases from a company without having to open account facilities	The quickest method of payment. Good for one off purchases	Good way of buying goods quickly, from a distance, or over the internet	Frequently used goods available immediatly. Items are bought in bulk and cheaper prices may apply
Against	Account facility needs to be set up in advance with each company. May be expected to use them regularly	Goods not dispatched until payment has been recieved	Security issues involving the cash and the staff. More paperwork involved than with most of the other methods of payment	Security and record keeping issues	Only for producing companies Needs the agreement of the finance department. Requires accurate record keeping from staff. Makes running expenditure figures more difficult to produce
Step 1	Order form completed (with prices) and signed	Order form completed (with prices) and signed	Production manager issued cash float by finance department	Supplier contacted or visited	Frequently used items bought in bulk using order form
Step 2	Expenditure recorded against show	Expenditure recorded against show	Production manager issues sub-floats to HODs	Credit card details given	Supplier paid.
Step 3	Order form taken to supplier or quoted over the phone	Order form taken to supplier or quoted over the phone	HODs visit suppliers (usually retail shops) and buy goods – suppler paid and **goods collected**	**Goods collected or dispatched**	**Departments sign for stock and can use immediately**
Step 4	**Goods collected or dispatched**	Invoice sent to finance department	HODs complete petty cash claim and take to Production Manager with reciepts and remaing cash	Expenditure recorded against show	Stock take carried out by Production manager once show opens
Step 5	Invoice sent to finance department	Payment approved by Production Manager	Production Manager completes pettycash claim, combining from several HODs	Monthly statement arrives for checking	Expenditure recorded against show
Step 6	Payment approved by Production Manager	Supplier paid	Expenditure recorded against show	Supplier paid via credit card company	
Step 7	Supplier paid	**Goods collected or dispatched**	Production Manager takes claim to finance department and has float reimbursed		

production manager may wish to issue a standard sheet to each HOD so that he can keep records of how their expenditure is going (*see* page 130).

Taxes such as VAT, GST or Sales Tax are not usually included in costings, so it is important that these are removed from expenditure records as well and that only the nett figure is quoted. In order for this to happen, finance departments will need to see invoices or receipts that include tax details.

Each department may also have a separate 'running budget' for maintaining its equipment and purchasing items that are not for any specific production. Again, records of expenditure should be kept.

Paying Staff

In a professional company there will also have to be systems in place for paying staff, freelance workers and casuals. Permanent staff will be working on a contract basis for a number of basic hours per week. They are also likely to earn some overtime as a result of exceeding their basic hours, missing meal breaks, or working late into the night. In fact it is almost impossible to mount a production without incurring overtime, especially once the show moves into the theatre, but the production manager needs to make sure they are in control of the cost of this overtime.

Both permanent and casual staff will be expected to complete a weekly timesheet that will be checked and signed by their HOD to confirm that they have worked the hours stated. It depends on the set-up of the theatre as to whether the HOD, the production manager or the finance department calculates the overtime. Whoever does the calculations will enter them onto a summary sheet prior to payment, and the production manager will want to check the amount and approve payment.

Overtime

As is the case with many of their other tasks, the production manager needs to be able to work out overtime quickly, even when very

RIGHT: *Production expenditure on a spreadsheet.*

OPPOSITE: *Different ways of paying for things.*

busy. The finance department will have a deadline by when they need to have information in order for people to be paid – and failing to be paid for overtime worked is not a happy situation. It may be in the middle of a fit-up or a technical rehearsal, but overtime figures still need to be produced.

One way of helping with this is to have staff fill in timesheets that indicate quickly and clearly the length of sessions they have worked, and the number of breaks they have taken. These can be devised to make the calculating of overtime straightforward.

Theatre employees work to a number of different union agreements and contracts, all of which will have different rules about hours of work, minimum salaries, overtime rates, breaks and working conditions. The production manager will need to understand the details and implications of each agreement so that they can be sure the right overtime payments are being made. It is a good idea to work out overtime requirements in advance with each HOD and agree a budget for each department; in that way the production manager will know how much is being spent, and the staff will know when they are expected to work. This will also ensure that laws such as the European Working Time Directive, which stipulates maximum hours of work and minimum breaks, are not being infringed.

Freelancers

There also need to be systems in place for the payment of freelance workers, and the theatre needs to be very careful of the tax situation. In order for the employer not to deduct tax, the freelancer needs to be registered as self employed – actors are nearly always classed as self employed, as are stage management, depending on the length of their

HOD expenditure form.

HODs Expenditure Record Sheet THIS PRODUCTION — Props Department

Date	Item	Supplier	Budget	Order Form Number	Amount	Cash Gross	Net	Credit Card Gross	Net	Items from Stock Number	Price	Nett	Totals	Budget Total spent Remaining
													£450.00	
													£301.70	
													£148.30	
01/05/01	Sanding belts	Parrys	£15.00	123810	£14.57								£14.57	
21/05/01	4mm ply	Stock	£40.00							5	£7.84	£39.20	£39.20	
21/05/01	Bolts	Flints	£6.00	123811	£6.40								£6.40	
21/05/01	Casting materials	Tirantis	£65.00	123814	£63.60								£63.60	
24/05/01	Pipe bender	Plant hire	£25.00					£23.50	£20.00				£20.00	
24/05/01	White emulsion	Stock	£10.00							1	£10.50	£10.50	£10.50	
08/06/01	Sink	DIY store	£120.00					£125.99	£107.22				£107.22	
09/06/01	Araldite	TDS Hardware	£4.00			£3.98	£3.39						£3.39	
09/06/01	Plumbing bits	Pro Plumb	£50.00			£43.27	£36.82						£36.82	

Production Department ___ **Equity Sub Rep Time Sheet**

Name _____ Production _____ Week Ending _____

	1	2	3	4	5	6	7	8	9	10	11	12	1	2	3	4	5	6	7	8	9	10	11	12	Basic	Double	1^½
Monday																											
Tuesday																											
Wednesday																											
Thursday																											
Friday																											
Saturday																											
Sunday																											

Overtime at Single (rounded up to full hour) _____

Sessions Over _____

Signed _____ Agreed (HOD) _____

Totals

Permitted Basic Hours

Overtime totals

Overtime Totals at single time

A blank timesheet. Staff cross through the time worked – each box represents 15 minutes.

contract. This means that they are responsible for their own tax affairs, and can deduct some professional expenses from their tax bill. Technicians are considered differently, and it is becoming more and more difficult for them to claim self-employed status because in theory you cannot be self-employed if you are told what to do or when to do it by a manager. This makes it difficult for theatres to employ freelancers within their building for long periods of time.

It is usual for freelancers to invoice the company for their work. The production manager may want to issue an order form to cover this, and to keep their good will they will want to be sure that freelancers get paid as quickly as possible.

SCHEDULING

The production manager will be concerned with several types of scheduling, and the ability to be accurate in time estimations, take all factors on board, think laterally, and be fair to everyone, are important production management skills.

Build and Paint Schedule

A schedule of the time allocated to build and paint each item of scenery needs to be produced in conjunction with the heads of construction, painting and possibly props or electrics. This should list:

• every item of the set;
• when it is to be built;

131

Production Departments			THIS PRODUCTION			Build and Paint Schedule
	Workshop		On floor	Paintshop	On Paintframe	Other
Date	Team 1	Team 2				
Week 1						
Mon 24 Mar	Previous show complete fit up		Previous show paint call			
Tue 25 Mar	Previous show notes		Previous show notes			
Wed 26 Mar	Previous show notes				Prime Florence cloth	
Thur 27 Mar	Cutting Lists	Cutting Lists			Paint Florence cloth	Previous show opens
Fri 28 Mar	Cutting Lists	Cutting Lists				
Week 2						
Mon 31 Mar	Door flat	Door and window				First rehearsal
Tue 1 Apr	Door flat to completion					MDF for floor delivered
Wed 2 Apr	Flattage 1		Door flat projection			Production meeting for next show
Thur 3 Apr						Progress meeting
Fri 4 Apr						Battens needed for canvasses
Week 3						
Mon 7 Apr	Flattage 2		Paint door flat		Canvasses onto frame	
Tue 8 Apr					Paint canvasses	
Wed 9 Apr	Ceiling					
Thur 10 Apr		Build up truck 1 in paintshop	Workshop building truck 1			Progress meeting
Fri 11 Apr						
Week 4						
Mon 14 Apr		Build up truck 2 in paintshop	Workshop building truck 2			
Tue 15 Apr			Paint trucks			
Wed 16 Apr			Paint trucks			
Thur 17 Apr	Slider frame	Slider frame				Progress meeting
Fri 18 Apr						
Week 5						**Production Schedule**
Sat 19 Apr	Strike previous show			Contingency time		Strike previous show/Rig LX
Sun 20 Apr	FIT UP			No call		Fit up this show/Rig LX FOH
Mon 21 Apr	Complete fit up					Fit up/Focus/Focus
Tue 22 Apr	Notes					Sound/Focus/Light/Light
Wed 23 Apr	Notes					**Tech/Tech/Tech**
Thu 24 Apr						**Tech/Tech/Dress**
Fri 25 Apr						**Tech work/Dress/OPEN**

An example of a build and paint schedule.

- when and where it is to be painted;
- the moving of items from one department to another;
- when items will be available for other departments, such as props, LX and sound to work on, and for the technical manager or crew to prepare it for flying.

This is quite a complex schedule, and there are many factors that need to be addressed; these include:

- the length of time needed for work on each item (which should be part of each department's costing);
- the complexity of the build process;
- the complexity of the painting work;
- the paint or texture drying time;
- keeping all departments occupied;
- the availability of materials (particularly the time needed to have backcloths or gauzes made up by the specialist supplier);
- the availability of space;
- the availability of staff;
- the order in which items will be needed at the fit-up;
- designer availability to approve finished work;
- other departments' involvement (LX, sound and props);
- any health and safety issues – for instance noise, dust, toxic materials.

It is best for the production manager to gather all this information from the HODs and then to produce a draft of the build and paint schedule. This can then be discussed with each department before publishing the agreed version.

Having fully consulted their HODs, the production manager has a right to expect that this schedule will be adhered to. Nevertheless, they will want to keep checking with HODs that things are going as planned so that, if necessary, changes can be negotiated with other departments. An agreement to some overtime may have to be made if departments fall behind the schedule. If they get ahead of schedule, this should not be used as a reason to slow down.

Production Schedule

In the early stages of planning for the production a rough breakdown of the time available in the theatre before the show opens will have been produced. This is a good starting-off point. The production manager now needs to produce a detailed breakdown of the work, in the form of the production schedule. This needs to cover, in the right sequence, every event from the closing of the previous show in the theatre to the first night of the new show. Ideally it should also include some contingency time.

Use of Stage Time

You should encourage the construction department to build and put together in the workshop as much of the set as possible, rather than leaving too much of it to the fit-up. Although there are things that it might be quicker to do when the set gets on stage, this will eat into precious stage time which you many want to prioritize for something else.

Another factor that will have been considered at the production meetings will be the painting of the floor. If the production is only playing in one theatre it may make sense to paint the stage floor (if this is permitted). Otherwise you will need to decide in conjunction with the designer and scenic artist how the floor finish is to be achieved. This could be by painting it onto hardboard or MDF, or onto a floorcloth that is fixed down at the fit-up.

A wet paint process like this on a floor would need extra time in the production schedule.

The production manager needs to start making decisions on how long each task is likely to take, in what order they need to happen for this particular show or design, and how many people need to be called upon and at what time. They should, as always, consult with their HODs and with the director, but it is often the case that the ideal amount of time is not available, and hard-nosed decisions need to be made that will allow the show to open on time without unduly compromising any one department's work or needs.

One of the problems with scheduling production week is dealing with the different union agreements, especially if working on a musical. For instance, technicians on BECTU contracts can work a five-hour session before they incur overtime, actors and stage management on Equity contracts can work four hours, but musicians on MU contracts can work only three hours. The production manager needs to decide what is the most efficient way of working and how much overtime can be afforded in order to make best use of the limited stage time available.

As with the build and paint schedule, the production manager should produce a draft of the production schedule. They should accept comment and input from the creative team and HODs, and continue to move jobs around and be creative about how the sessions can be used until the final schedule is agreed and published. However, even in production week, the production manager needs to be ready to amend the schedule.

Scheduling of Other Departments

It is usual for departments that work largely on their own, such as wardrobe, props, LX and sound, to produce their own schedules for completing work up to the start of production week. The production manager will still want assurance that these departments are on target for everything to be ready at the appropriate point in production week, and will expect – indeed, will insist – on being informed of any problems that departments encounter in sticking to their schedule.

PROGRESS MEETINGS

These are a vital bringing-together of the key players involved in putting on productions. For a show that is rehearsing full time, they should be held once a week (before rehearsals start in the morning is a good time). For other rehearsal time-scales, the production manager will need to decide how often to call progress meetings.

As with all production-related matters, the production manager will chair this meeting. Progress meetings are pointless without the director, designer and the DSM present, and all HODs should attend (or send a representative with authority to make decisions on their behalf). Ideally the lighting designer, sound designer and, if used, musical director and choreographer will also be present.

It is a good idea to prepare a loose agenda for these meetings, and distribute it in advance. In doing this the production manager should start with any issues that they feel need addressing, then read through all the rehearsal notes published since the last meeting and make a list of any questions that need to be answered, points that need to be noted, or additional items of work that need to be agreed. It is important to get decisions at the meeting, and not just to read through the notes.

An example of a progress meeting agenda.

THIS PRODUCTION
Progress Meeting Agenda

Date:	Tuesday 18th September
Venue:	Meeting Room
Time:	9.00am

1. Points from Rehearsal Notes

General
• Decision on the position of the interval
• Tickertape machine
• Run throughs

New Props
• Bench
• Calculators
• Newspapers
• Briefcase
• Magazines
• Smoking (How much)
• Large tray with lipped edge for champagne
• Champagne glasses
• Water cooler

Production
• Steps to upper level
• Availability of stock rostra
• Champagne glasses construction

Wardrobe
• Change of skirt and tie for Mr Ashton for scene 5
• Pockets needed in all overcoats
• Additional fitting required for Miss Mercer
• Rehearsal skirts

New Sound Qs
• Taxi
• Background announcements

LX
Practical lamp on each desk

2. Finalised Production Schedule

3. Health and Safety

• Discuss draft risk assessment
• Discuss champagne glasses and spillages
• Availability of flame and smoking plots

4. Progress Report, Queries, Concerns or Requirements from each Department

5. AOB

Date of next meeting Tuesday 25th September 2001, Studio theatre, at 9.00am.

Each individual should be allowed to raise any issues that are not on the agenda and which they feel need discussing, points they want clarifying, decisions they need to obtain, or things they need to schedule. Progress meetings are also an excellent opportunity to discuss issues such as the production schedule. When it is intended to do this, everyone involved should have a copy in advance so they can study it and bring their comments to the meeting. As with all meetings, the production manager should close the progress meeting by announcing the date, time and venue of the next meeting.

PREPARING FOR PRODUCTION WEEK

The whole focus of the production manager's work while a show is in rehearsal is towards being ready for production week. They need to be sure that absolutely everything needed for the show is being made, altered, bought or hired by one of the departments.

When a theatre is not putting on performances, it is known as being 'dark'. Due to the need to earn money through the box office, every theatre company wants to keep this dark period as short as possible, and so there will never be as much time as everyone would like to fit up and

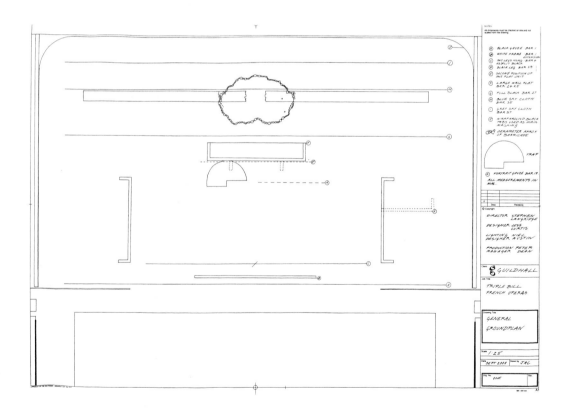

The original groundplan for a production. Designer: Jessica Curtis.

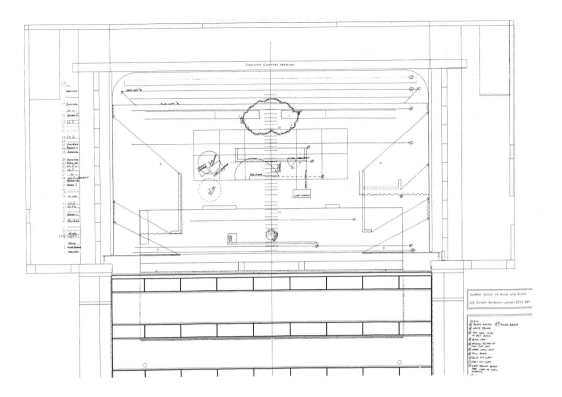

The same groundplan as added to by production management.

rehearse the show in the theatre. To reduce the pressure that this causes, it is important to ensure that as much as possible is done in advance.

Depending on the scale of the organization, production management may have items for which they are responsible. They should not allow these to fall behind due to other pressures or because of the amount of time they have to spend facilitating and problem solving. They will particularly want to be sure that the groundplan is up to date and comprehensive. We saw in Chapter 4 that the groundplan is produced by the designer in time for the first production meeting. This will be several weeks before the fit-up, so it is unlikely that all the information on the plan will still be up to date by production week. The ground plan must be constantly updated either

by the production manager (in conjunction with the designer and lighting designer), or delegated to others, for instance the technical manager.

Everyone should remember that the groundplan is a working document for everyone: it is not just the designer's property or work, and can be regarded as a map for the fit-up. Items to consider for the final groundplan include:

- the accurate position of all flown pieces;
- the structure that it has been agreed is necessary to hold up the set, but which is not on the original plan;
- get-off or access stairs;
- flown LX bars and vertical LX bars, known as booms (once the final LX plan is delivered);
- masking – though this can only be finalized

137

Maximum bar loading 252kg

	Date 24.9.01

THE PLAYHOUSE. HANGING PLOT

BAR	DISTANCE FROM PROS	SHOW: *Last Production*	Weight in kg	No of Weights	Changeover Notes	SHOW: *This Production*	Weight in kg	No of Weights	BAR
BACK WALL	9.96								BACK WALL
34A	HEMP 9.06			*hemp set*				*hemp set*	34A
34	8.86	Hedge cut out & LX	180	15		Backcloth	72	6	34
33	8.66	Star cloth (stored)	78	6	*stays*	Star cloth (stored)	78	6	33
30B	HEMP 8.46			*hemp set*				*hemp set*	30B
30A	HEMP 8.26			*hemp set*				*hemp set*	30A
30	8.06	LX 7 inc IWB	204	17	*IWB stays*	LX 4	180	15	30
28A	HEMP 7.86			*hemp set*				*hemp set*	28A
28	7.66	LX 6	144	12		Border 4	180	15	28
27A	HEMP 7.46			*hemp set*				*hemp set*	27A
27	7.17	Window	192	16					27
26	6.97	Top of back wall	120	10					26
25B	HEMP 6.77	Border		*hemp set*	*stays*	Border (stored)		*hemp set*	25B
25A	HEMP 6.57			*hemp set*				*hemp set*	25A
25	6.24	LX 5 (backlight)	216	18		LX 3 (backlight)	180	15	25
24	6.04	Border	36	3	*to bar 28*				24
23	5.84								23
22	5.64	Door frame	96	8		Border 3	36	3	22
20A	HEMP 5.44			*hemp set*				*hemp set*	20A
20	5.24	Fireplace	252	21					20
19A	HEMP 5.04			*hemp set*				*hemp set*	19A
19	4.84	Border	39	3	*to bar 22*				19
18	4.64	Stag painting	24	2					18
17	4.44	Flowers painting	24	2		LX 2	144	12	17
15A	HEMP 4.24			*hemp set*				*hemp set*	15A
15	4.04								15
14	3.84	Border	36	3	*stays*	Border (stored)	36	3	14
13	3.64	LX 4	192	16		Flown set	180	15	13
12B	HEMP 3.44			*hemp set*				*hemp set*	12B
12A	HEMP 3.24	Border		*hemp set*		Border 2		*hemp set*	12A
12	2.91								12
11	2.69	Leaf drop 2	12	1					11
10	2.43	Leaf drop 1	12	1					10
9	2.2								9
8	2	LX 3	168	14					8
6A	HEMP 1.80			*hemp set*				*hemp set*	6A
6	1.6	Gauze	24	2					6
5	1.4	Border	36	3	*to bar 1*	LX 1	234	18	5
4	1.09	Speaker	24	2					4
3	0.94	LX 2	216	18	*IWB stays*	IWB stored	65	5	3
2	0.7					Front cloth	39	3	2
1	0.5	LX 1 inc IWB	264	22	*IWB to 5*	House border (1)	39	3	1

once LX requirements are known, and should be agreed in conjunction with the lighting designer;
- sight lines;
- items from stock that may differ in size from the ones the designer originally drew;
- offstage as well as onstage positions of scenery, and large items of furniture or props (so it is known where everything will live in the wings and that there is enough space);
- areas in the wings such as quick change areas and clear routes to fire exits or fire-fighting equipment;
- the revised position of anything that has changed during rehearsals;
- large items of sound equipment, for instance speakers;
- adjusting the position of some items to allow clearance for pieces that move;
- an issue number and date, to ensure that everyone is working from the most up-to-date information.

Preparing for the Fit-Up

To save time at the fit-up, the production manager should discuss its order, in advance, with the construction manager, the technical manager and the chief LX. They should go through the fit-up in their head to make sure they know how it is going to run, and that the agreed order will work. They must also complete and distribute the risk assessment, and have a meeting with the staff involved regarding the order, timing and safety of the fit-up.

The relevant departments should do the following:

- Identify all stock items, check that they are in good working order, and get them as close to the stage as possible.
- Pre-rig any flown pieces if the previous show allows it.

OPPOSITE: *An example of hanging plot.*

Hanging Plot

This is a list of what is to be hung on each flying bar. This should also include:
- the up and downstage position of the bar relative to a fixed point, such as the front of the stage or the back of the safety curtain
- what is on the bar in the previous show
- if this is a stock item (e.g, a border or pre-wired lighting bar), where it moves to
- the weight of the item(s) on the bar in both pounds or kilos and in number of weights. There are programs that will calculate the weight of LX bars: the weight of scenic items should be calculated as part of the manual handling assessment, and the weight of stock items will already be known
- the maximum loading allowed on each bar
- notes about anything specific for each piece
- the height at which each bar has to be (known as 'the dead')
- any bars being used for storage

- Install or move any pulleys, motors or other special rigging in the grid.
- Check, lubricate and fit castors on any trucks.
- Cut to length, and if necessary paint black, any scaffolding tube needed for rigging or for steeldeck legs.
- Although scenery will need to be in sections for moving it onto stage, it should have been fitted together in the workshop and stacked in the right order ready for the fit-up.
- Label all scenery, so that everyone knows which piece is which.
- Put a weight indication on every piece of scenery so that people know how heavy it is, and to comply with manual handling regulations.

- Make sure the model and copies of the up-to-date version of the groundplan are available (pieces of the model may need collecting from different departments, who have been using it as reference).
- Make sure all tools and equipment needed for the fit-up are available and working.
- Check there is a stock of all the hardware needed (screws and nails, nuts and bolts, flying tackle) in all necessary sizes.
- Fix all flying tackle and cables to each piece of scenery, so they only have to be attached to the bar at the fit-up (*see* below).
- Write on the back of the piece of scenery the distance of each cable from the centre line of the stage to save measuring at the fit-up.

- Check all access equipment for safety (these checks must be recorded in a log).
- Get the stage area as clear as possible, and empty all rubbish bins.
- Have equipment available for moving heavy items of scenery, and check it for correct working.

Preparing for the Technical Rehearsal

The technical rehearsal is the point at which all the prepared elements of a production are put together and fine-tuned to make sure they work safely and in conjunction with each other. It is the first time that the performers get on stage and the show is worked through in sequence, getting every aspect right.

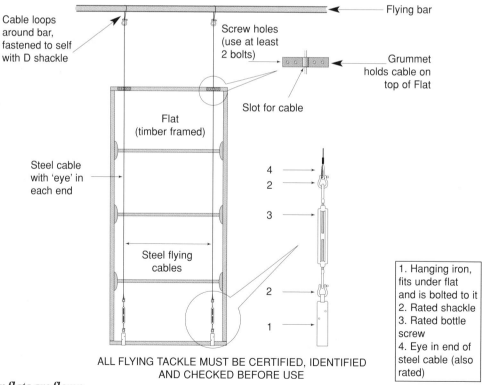

How flats are flown.

It is at the technical rehearsal that anyone's lack of planning really comes to light. It is important for everyone to realize that this is not the time for inventing what has to happen in a show, working out how effects can be achieved, or even how individual items can be made to work.

The production manager needs to make sure they know what all the individual elements are, and how they are going to function singly and together. Throughout the production process they need to instil in their staff and creative team (especially the director) their philosophy about having everything ready for the tech.

Stage management, in conjunction with the production manager and other departments, will be preparing setting and running lists detailing exactly how the show will work. As described in chapter six, there will be a chance to check all planning and paperwork at the final run through in the rehearsal room.

Particular attention needs to be paid to the sequence of scenery and furniture changes, and to offstage storage. A good way of doing this is to use a groundplan and the pieces from the model, and to work through the show in miniature.

PROBLEM SOLVING

It is impossible for a production manager to predict all of the problems they and their team will encounter while preparing and rehearsing a production, although as they gain experience they may be able to anticipate some of them.

The production manager should not sit in their office and wait for people to seek them out with problems: whenever possible they should visit each production department at

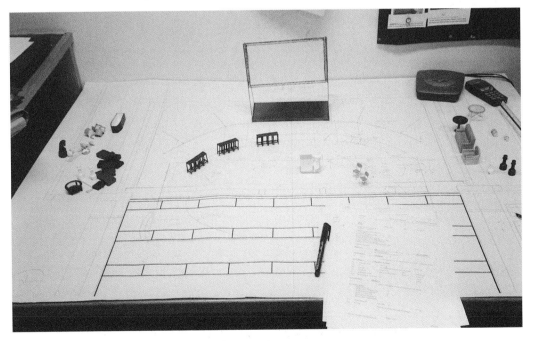

Working out scene changes in miniature.

Listening to Problems

When anyone comes to you with their problems, you should try to behave as follows:

- stay calm;
- let the member of staff get to the end of what they have to say;
- make sure you fully understand the problem, and evaluate its consequences;
- not try to apportion blame (at least not now);
- thank the person for sharing the problem with you;
- ask them what they see as the solution;
- take a balanced overview (the person presenting the problem may only see it from their point of view);
- involve others whom the problem affects;
- decide whether you need to solve the problem immediately, or have a little time;
- think about other possible, less obvious solutions (lateral thinking)

Many of the above are standard management techniques that you can apply to other situations.

least twice a day. This need not be a formal thing, but they will be able to observe quite a lot of things:

- how the work is progressing;
- whether a department is on schedule;
- how different pieces of the production are going to fit together;
- whether staff are following health and safety guidelines;
- what the morale of the department is like;
- how well individuals and departments are working together.

As discussed earlier, it is also a good idea for the production manager to drop in on rehearsals and to visit the stage management office regularly.

It is important for everyone to realize that the production manager is there to solve problems, that they see this as an important part of their job, and regard problems as a challenge not as an obstacle. All staff should feel comfortable in being able to identify, anticipate and bring problems to the production manager, although normally this will be via the HOD. How the production manager reacts to being presented with a problem will influence staff willingness to share their problems.

CONCLUSION

In this chapter we have looked at the production manager's involvement with facilitating the rehearsing and building of a show, and his or her preparations for moving the show into the theatre. The next chapter deals with the production week itself, and the production manager's involvement as making the show happen becomes a reality.

8 THE PRODUCTION WEEK

Production week is the time when the production manager's weeks of planning are put to the test. Nothing should have been left to chance, and everything should have been thought through and discussed with those who are actually doing the work. How efficiently a production manager operates during production week can make a huge difference to how long everything takes.

What's Plan B?

The production manager should always have a 'plan B', to cope with as many difficult situations and problems as he/she can anticipate: for instance, a worried designer whose set does not work as intended, or a director when a production begins to run out of time in production week. These plans are likely to involve the use of financial contingencies in terms of paying for more overtime, additional staff or equipment.

What happens during any production week varies according to the set-up of the theatre or organization, and the requirements of the show, and the following description can only be an overview. For an amateur production manager, or one who is working for a production company, the production week starts when the theatre becomes available to the company. For a building-based production manager it starts at curtain down of the final performance of the previous show, when the first task will be striking the set, props, furniture and costumes from the stage. Depending on the scale of the show, this may take anything from a few hours to a few days. An example of a production week schedule is shown on the next page.

Production managers, indeed most theatre staff, can expect little life outside the theatre during production week: it is an all-consuming process. It is important, however, that everyone, including the production manager, takes sufficient breaks and eats properly during this time. It is also important to ensure that routine tasks do not fall too far behind: staff still need paying, and they will continue to need petty cash and orders for last-minute purchases. There may be urgent work to do on forthcoming productions, and phone calls that need returning.

RIGGING LX

Unless the theatre has a fixed lighting rig, the first task for the new show will be to rig the flown LX onstage. This needs to happen first so that it is out of the way before the set starts to be fitted up. The production manager does not need to be around while rigging is happening, it can be left in the hands of the chief LX and their team, plus a crew on the fly floor to fly the bars and load the counterweights.

Rigging involves a major amount of physical work, and is likely to involve a large crew to get

Saturday 19 April

am	Run through in the rehearsal room
2.00	Matinee Previous show
7.15	Final performance Previous show
10.00pm	De rig LX and Get out Previous show and **rig flown LX for This Production**

Sunday 20 April

9.00	**Fit up** This Production – masking then flown set then flattage
1.00	Lunch
2.00	Continue fit up
7.00	Tea
7.00	Workshop, crew and casuals finish Paint the floor LX rig FOH
11.00pm	Latest finish for LX

Monday 21 April

9.00	Continue fit up Rig sound Stage management doing returns from Previous Show
10.00	LX rig practicals
12.00	Deading session
1.00	Lunch Sound systems check
2.00	**Focusing (1)**
pm & eve	Rehearsals in the rehearsal room for company and extras
6.00	Tea
7.00	**Continue focusing (2)**
	After rehearsals clear rehearsal room
12.00 midnight	Latest finish for LX

Tuesday 22 April

am	Possible calls for fittings, haircuts etc.
9.00	**Sound plotting** (director needed) Props and stage management set dressing
11.00	**Continue focusing (3)** nb short session
1.00	Lunch Possible workshop notes
pm	Possible line run
2.00	**Lighting (1)** Stage Management set up for Tech
6.00	Tea
7.00	**Continue lighting (2)**
10.00pm	Call ends

Wednesday 23 April

9.25	Half hour call
10.00	**Introduction and Safety Talk** on stage
then	**Technical rehearsal (1)**
1.00	Lunch
2.00	Cast called to get back into costume
2.15	**Continue Technical Rehearsal (2)**
5.30	Tea
6.30	Company called back
6.45	**Continue Technical Rehearsal (3)**
10.15	Rehearsal ends
10.30	Call ends Possible paint call (to be confirmed)

Thursday 24 April

9.00	Lighting or Technical work
9.30	Half hour call
10.00	**Continue Technical Rehearsal (4)**
12.45	Company break
1.00	Lunch
2.00	Half hour call
2.35	**Continue Technical Rehearsal (3)** or run through
5.30	Tea
6.55	Half hour call
7.30	**Dress Rehearsal 1** (photographer present)
After dress	Technical notes

Friday 25 April

am	Technical Work as required Company called for notes
12.55	Company lunch
1.55	Half hour call
2.30	Dress Rehearsal 2 followed by notes
6.55	half hour call
7.30	**First Performance This Production**
After show	First Night Buffet in the Upper Foyer

Saturday 26 February

pm	Possible calls for notes
7.30	**Performance This Production**

Peter Dean
Production Manager

Distribution: Chief Exec, Director, Designer, Costume Designer, Lighting Designer, Sound Designer, Production Manager, Production Assistant, Stage Manager, DSM, ASMs, Chief LX, Board Op, Sound, Technical Manager, Stage Crew, Workshop, Paintshop, Props, Wardrobe Supervisor, Wardrobe, Dressers, Marketing Manager, Theatre Manager, Stage Door staff (27)
Notice Boards: Production, Green Room, Rehearsal Room, Dressing Room corridor, Stage Door (5)

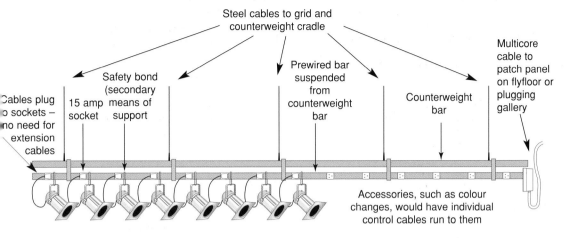

Steel cables to grid and
counterweight cradle

Multicore
cable to
patch panel
on flyfloor or
plugging
gallery

Safety bond
(secondary
means of
support)

Prewired bar
suspended
from
counterweight
bar

Counterweight
bar

15 amp
socket

Cables plug
o sockets –
no need for
extension
cables

Accessories, such as colour
changes, would have individual
control cables run to them

ABOVE: A diagram of how an LX bar works.

OPPOSITE: An example of a production schedule.

it done as quickly as possible: these are likely to be a mixture of the resident LX staff, and experienced and inexperienced casuals. (For the sequence of rigging and de-rigging lighting bars, *see* page 99.)

As the aim of production week is the efficient use of time, it may not be necessary for LX to complete the rigging at this stage. They need to do enough to be clear of the stage area when the set is being fitted up. By the time focusing starts, however, every lantern must have been rigged, checked for working and plugged into its designated circuit.

Once LX have rigged, the schedule may call for the scenic artist(s) to begin to paint the floor: as already discussed in Chapter 7, how and when this happens can be crucial to the planning of the fit-up.

Fitting-up

Once the floor has been painted and the paint has dried, it is time to start the fit-up. This is when the production manager is likely to first appear on stage with everything they need.

This includes their production file containing all the paperwork for the production, the groundplan, side elevation, a scale rule and a large notepad. They should already be wearing safety shoes, and should also bring their hard hat and, possibly, ear defenders and work gloves. The work will be done by the construction manager and the technical manager and their teams, with the production manager overseeing and co-ordinating.

All the flown pieces must be rigged first, and the best way to do this is to work logically through the hanging plot, rigging all the

---

Painting the Floor

There are several factors to bear in mind about this operation:

• What is on the floor already?
• Will this take a lot of painting out?
• How many processes will it take to achieve the desired paint effect?
• What is the drying time of each process?
• Will there need to be a further paint call to tie in the floor with the rest of the set?
• Can you avoid damage to the newly painted floor during the fit-up?

Painting a floor.

masking and any stock tabs first. Some may already be rigged from the previous show, but will probably be in the wrong place: the hanging plot will indicate what must be moved. It saves a lot of confusion if there is the facility on the fly floor to label each bar with what is on it, and the fly crew must keep this constantly updated. Next, fly the flown pieces of the set. Once this is done, double check that everything that needs to be flown has been, and then start fitting up the set itself. Again, this will be different for every single show.

The production manager's job at this point is to co-ordinate everybody's work, and to make sure that everyone is fully occupied, and that they are working safely. They should keep themselves free from any specific jobs, but should also lead from the front if there are heavy pieces to move or jobs that everyone

needs to be involved in. All those working on the fit-up, particularly casuals, should be divided into teams as part of planning the fit-up. Team leaders should make sure that everyone has a job and knows what it is, and who they are working for. The production manager will want to know when jobs are finished, if people are lacking in information about what needs doing, and if they hit a problem.

It is important to double check that the set is being put up in the right place. This is not because of a lack of trust in the work of the designer or in the measuring skills of the technical or construction staff, but because mistakes can happen, and it can be very embarrassing and expensive to have to move the completed set when it is realized at the end of the day that scenery is obstructing the safety curtain or does not line up with a flown piece, or that lighting equipment is in the wrong place relative to the set. The first few measurements, which perhaps determine where the floor starts, are the most crucial. The production manager should particularly check that everyone is working from the same datum point on the groundplan and on the stage.

The fit-up is likely to take several hours, if not days, and the production manager should take responsibility for calling drinks breaks and meal breaks.

In managing the fit-up it is good practice to:

• set a target for each team in each session.
• encourage a piece of work to be finished by announcing that there will be a break once it is done.
• make sure that everyone returns promptly at the end of a break, as the theatre does not want to be paying people for taking extended breaks.
• at the end of a heavy day's fit-up, if the schedule permits it, call a slightly early finish, raid the petty cash tin and take everyone to the pub. Drinking alcohol during breaks between work sessions should, however, be actively discouraged for safety reasons.

By the end of the fit-up, everything has to be ready for the next activity, which is likely to be focusing. If the LX rig was not completed prior to the fit-up, the LX crew will return at some point and rig equipment front of house, on booms and on the set itself. However, this should not be allowed to interfere with the work of fitting up the set. The final two parts of the fit-up are to set positions for all flown scenery, masking and lighting, and to start the jobs list in conjunction with the construction manager and technical manager.

Jobs Lists

These lists are an important way for the production manager to check that everything that needs to happen for a show does actually happen. They should start the production week with a list of everything that needs to happen at the fit-up, and cross the jobs off as they are completed. At the end of the fit-up they should liaise with their HODs about any outstanding items, alterations that need to be made, or problems that need to be solved. If possible, they should estimate how long these will take, and start to think about where there is time in the schedule for them to happen. It may be that departments will have some preparatory work to do before needing time on stage.

As well as the jobs the production manager notices or knows about, there will also be jobs from the creative team, particularly the set designer. These need to be allocated to the relevant department, and time scheduled for them to be completed.

It is best to keep the master copy of the jobs list on the production desk, either on a laptop computer or a paper copy, so that it can be constantly updated. The list should state what the deadline is for each job to be completed – for instance, before lighting, before the tech, before photographs, before the first night – and which department is responsible for the job (*see* example on next page).

The Deading Session

The setting of positions for flown pieces is an important, and sometimes overlooked, part of the fit-up: it is known as the 'deading session'.

The production manager should co-ordinate the deading session and, like many things they do, if well organized it can be quite quick, if not it can drag on and even result in changes being necessary later in the production process. It is therefore described in some detail on the next few pages.

Getting things right at this stage can avoid a lot of problems later. Exact positions of items of scenery, lighting and masking should

Opera Triple Bill Jobs List. Monday 30th November

Paintshop	Paint front of stage black	By first dress rehearsal
Workshop	Tidy edges of trap pallet	Before paint call
Crew	Gauze holes need repairing	By first dress rehearsal
LX	Lower LX bar on pit rail	Before focusing
Crew	Move winch control to fly floor	Before scene change rehearsal (Tues am)
Crew	Black flat SL catching on iron	Today
Workshop	Turn buckles for pallet storage	Before scene change rehearsal
Crew	Change conduit border 5	Before focusing
Workshop	Holes for sliding handrails at top of stairs	Before stage and piano 1
Crew	Secure guard rails in pit SR	Before sitzprobe
Workshop	Get side walls upright (spirit level)	Before focusing
Sound	Another Q light in LX box	By first dress rehearsal
Crew	Sleeve for chain hoist chain	By first dress rehearsal
Workshop	Complete window piece	Today
Paintshop	Paint window piece	Once completed by workshop
Crew	Kick rail pit front	Before stage and piano 1
LX	Boom barriers	Before stage and piano 1

L'Enfant (1st Opera)

Props	Cut mat to size	Before focusing
Props	Linen drape needs ironong	By first dress
Props	Pole for hanging drape	By scene change rehearsal
Paintshop	Creases out of blue cloth	By first dress
SM	Dolly for water container	Before scene change rehearsal

Portrait de Manon (2nd Opera)

Crew	Check masking to hide portrait	Before lighting
Workshop	Window is hinge bound and need a latch	Before stage and piano 1
Crew	Put cable ties on frame flying cables	By first dress
Workshop	Reveal onto pallet then revise lifting mechanism	By scene change rehearsal
Crew	Turn split black back	Before focusing
Crew	? Extend side masking	(to be discussed with designer and LD)
Paintshop	Paint star rail pewter colour	Before first dress rehearsal
Workshop	Straighten star rail	Before first dress rehearsal
Workshop	Fix handrail substage	Before stage and piano 1
SM	White gaffer treads	Before stage and piano 1
LX	Slides need finalising	Before lighting
SM	Foam under pallet to stop heads being banged	Before stage and piano 1

La Navarraise (Final Opera)

Props	Fix down tree	Before scene change rehearsal
Props	Paint ammo boxes	By first dress

Today's Schedule

9.00 – 10.00	Technical work and set up for sitzprobe
10.00 – 1.00	**Sitzprobe** (quiet on stage)
1.00 – 2.00	Technical work and set up L'enfant for focusing
2.00 – 6.00	**Focusing**
6.00 – 7.00	Change to Portrait de Manon
7.00 – 10.00	**Focusing**
10.00pm	**Paint call** on the floor

Deads (UK) and Trims (US)

A dead is both the position of an item or piece of scenery, and the indication (usually a piece of coloured tape) that marks that position.

For a flown piece, the dead is marked on the rope on the fly floor; for a piece of scenery on stage it is marked, discretely, on the floor.

If a flown piece does not move during a production, it is still important to mark its position. This would be known as a 'permanent dead'.

On stage we do not refer to flying bars as moving up or down but as flying *in* or *out* (from being 'in view' or 'out of view'). So a dead for the lower position of a flying piece is known as the 'in dead', and the dead for its higher position as the 'out dead'.

In the US, a dead for a flown piece is called a 'trim', and a tape mark on the floor a 'spike'.

have been agreed in advance between the production manager, the set designer and the lighting designer, and should be shown on the side elevation. Bar heights can also be written on the hanging plot. Nevertheless this can only be a theoretical exercise, and the reality of what a piece of masking actually does, or the angle of a specific light, may lead to changes being necessary.

The following staff should be available:

• The fly crew on the fly floor to fly bars (with hanging plot and tape to mark deads).
• An additional fly crew to clear any bars that foul on each other, and to adjust the weighting of counterweight bars.

OPPOSITE: An example of a jobs list.

• Electricians to make sure that enough slack cable is available for each LX bar to move.
• A crew on stage with either a long pole with measurements marked on it, or a long tape measure and access equipment to get to the flying bars, so that the height of the bars above the stage can be measured.
• A crew on stage to clear any obstructions and move any required pieces of scenery into place.

Brailing

Quite often a lighting bar, or a piece of scenery or masking will not be in exactly the right place, despite being rigged on the correct bar. This can be corrected by a process known as brailing.

Either a piece of rope is tied to the end of the flying bar and tied to the fly rail to adjust the position of the flown piece, or a rope is stretched between fly floors and used to pull the whole bar up- or downstage. This is a better method as it keeps the bar straighter, and the bar can be moved in and out a little without releasing the line. Technically this should be called 'breasting'.

If a bar needs to fly right in or out and still be brailed, a running brail needs to be used. This is a tight vertical rope running from the grid to the stage floor near each end of the bar, which the flying bar runs against.

It is important that the position of brail or breast lines are marked where they are tied to the fly floor, so that if they need to be removed for some reason, the brailed position of the bar can be accurately recreated (*see* diagram page 154).

The production manager should sit in the first or second row of the stalls. If the rows curve, they should be at one end, as this will be the worst seat from which to make the masking work. If possible, the production manager should be in communication with the flyman via headsets or radio, and if these are not available, they will have to ask for quiet on stage. The designer and lighting designer should also be present.

The production manager will need their copy of the hanging plot, a side elevation and scale rule. It should be remembered that this will be the first time that the designer has seen the set on stage and they may start to give notes about changes needed.

The way in which to determine deads will be different for each design: some will need to be set visually, some to the measured heights that have been worked out from the side elevation and which should now be on the hanging plot. It is usually best to start with the furthest upstage piece; the front border (known as the house border) will also be the key in determining some deads.

The following sequence of diagrams, which also relates to the hanging plot on page 138, shows one possible sequence of what the production manager would ask for and look for in running a deading session.

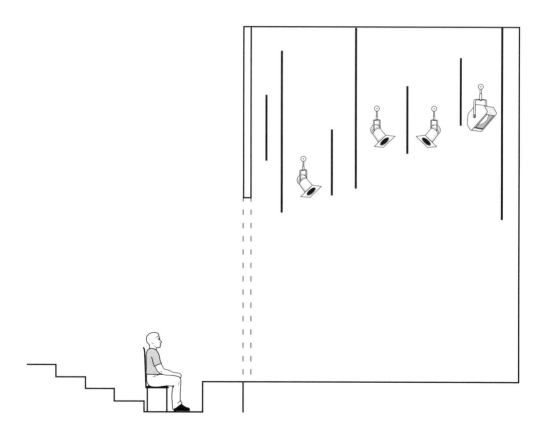

Start with a clear stage with everything flown out.

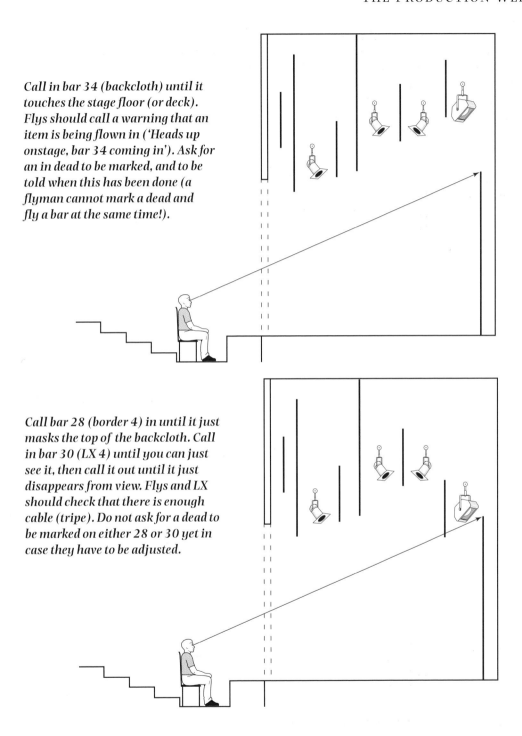

Call in bar 34 (backcloth) until it touches the stage floor (or deck). Flys should call a warning that an item is being flown in ('Heads up onstage, bar 34 coming in'). Ask for an in dead to be marked, and to be told when this has been done (a flyman cannot mark a dead and fly a bar at the same time!).

Call bar 28 (border 4) in until it just masks the top of the backcloth. Call in bar 30 (LX 4) until you can just see it, then call it out until it just disappears from view. Flys and LX should check that there is enough cable (tripe). Do not ask for a dead to be marked on either 28 or 30 yet in case they have to be adjusted.

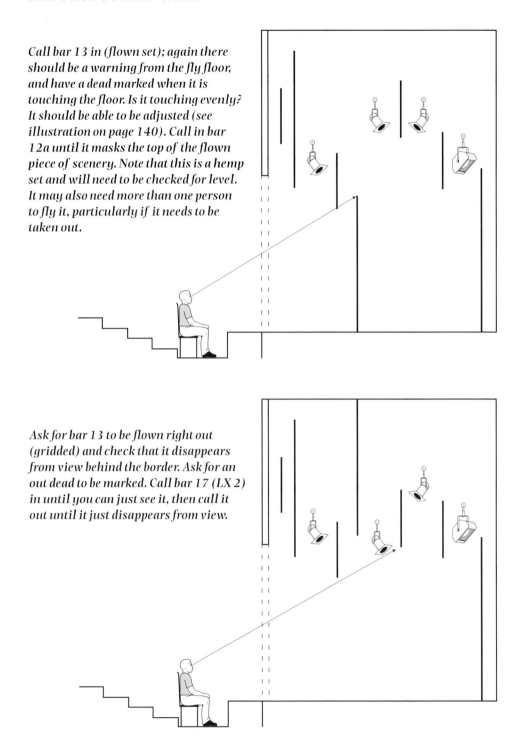

Call bar 13 in (flown set); again there should be a warning from the fly floor, and have a dead marked when it is touching the floor. Is it touching evenly? It should be able to be adjusted (see illustration on page 140). Call in bar 12a until it masks the top of the flown piece of scenery. Note that this is a hemp set and will need to be checked for level. It may also need more than one person to fly it, particularly if it needs to be taken out.

Ask for bar 13 to be flown right out (gridded) and check that it disappears from view behind the border. Ask for an out dead to be marked. Call bar 17 (LX 2) in until you can just see it, then call it out until it just disappears from view.

Ask to have bar 2 (the front cloth) flown in (safety call again from flys) and have an in dead marked. Call bar 1 (house border) in, and dead it where it just masks the top of the front cloth.

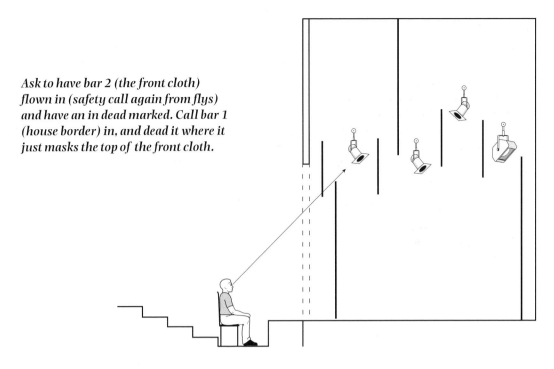

Ask to have bar 2 flown out until it just disappears from view. Have an out dead marked at this point (there is no need to take it to the grid, if it is just out of view it will appear without delay when any cue to fly it in is given). Border 3 (bar 22) does not relate to any particular piece of scenery and should be deaded where it is drawn on the side elevation. If you have not already noted it, measure this on your side elevation and get the crew to measure the height of the bottom of the border and fly the bar in or out until the measurement is right. Dead the LX backlight bar (counterweight 25) just out of view, but check with the lighting designer that they can light as far downstage as they need to from this bar. If this is a problem, taking border 3 and the LX bar out will help.

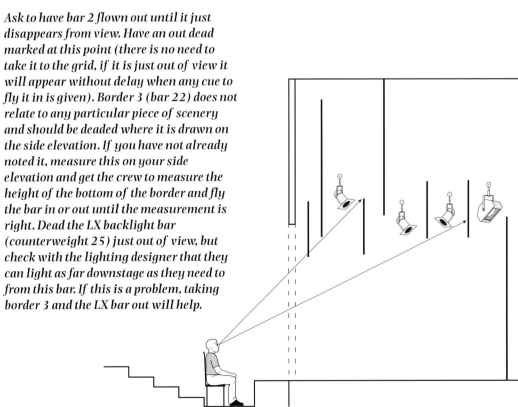

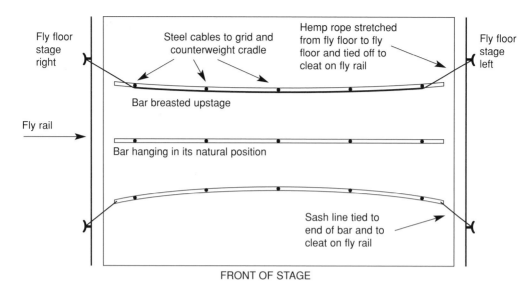

FRONT OF STAGE

Diagram of brailing and breasting viewed from above. See also 'Brailing' on page 149

Once the lighting designer and the designer are happy with the positions of all the flown items, the flyman should be asked to mark the deads on all LX bars and borders, and to double check that everything else is marked. Ask the LX crew to haul up any excess cables (known as 'tripe').

During this deading process, the flyman should be checking that each bar that he or she moves is properly balanced, and should be adjusting the weight as required. The rest of the staff who have been called for the fit-up should be clearing up, putting tools away, and sweeping the stage ready for electrics to start focusing.

FOCUSING

With the set in place, LX can turn the working lights out and start the process of focusing. This means getting to each lantern and, under instruction from the lighting designer, making it do the job that was intended when the lighting plan was drawn.

The production manager's role here is to ensure that as much as possible is ready for focusing – that all the lights are rigged, and the set and masking are complete – and that there is quiet to enable everyone to concentrate and communicate easily. Stage management should have transferred the positions of any furniture from the mark-up in the rehearsal room to the stage itself, and have the actual furniture available so that any specials (lanterns with specific functions) can be focused on it. If available, it is a good idea to have the director and designer check these positions before focusing starts. Stage management should be on call to set furniture and answer any queries that the lighting designer may have about positions of furniture, props, actors and action.

Lighting designers differ as to where they like to start focusing. Some like to start front of house and work their way forwards until they reach the furthest upstage bar; others like to start upstage and finish up front of house. Booms, stands and lights on the set itself are usually focused last. There will also be considerations for the production manager if the show has several scenes: for instance, does the designer intend to focus all the general lighting and then come back to the lanterns that are specific to each scene, or are the crew going to have to be available to move scenery throughout focusing? It is also useful to know how the lighting designer intends to work, as this can affect who is called when, how the stage needs to be left at the end of the fit-up, and whether any work other than focusing can be carried out. If there is to be other work going on at this time it must be quiet, as concentration and easy communication are needed for focusing; and it must be able to be done in the dark, as the working lights will be turned off for focusing.

The sequence of focusing each lantern, depending on its type, will be to:

- get it pointing in the right general direction;
- change the size of the beam of light;
- make it hard- or soft-edged;
- cut it off from hitting parts of the stage or set which it is not supposed to light;
- make sure that any gobos (see below) are creating the desired image;

Gobo

A gobo is a patterned metal (or, more expensively, glass) disc that can be used in profile lanterns to produce patterns on stage.

Examples include leaf patterns, light coming through windows, clouds or geometric shapes.

There are frequently used gobos which most theatres carry in stock or which can be bought from suppliers. Lighting designers can also specify their own designs and have them specially made.

Turning Lights Off

It is important that everyone onstage, including those in the wings, is warned before working lights are turned off, so that they are not plunged unexpectedly into darkness. A shout of 'workers going out' is therefore given by the person switching working lights off.

It is equally important that there is a warning during lighting sessions and the technical rehearsal before going to a blackout or very dark lighting state. Either the board operator or lighting designer needs to call out 'going dark on stage' before this happens.

Part of the risk assessment should be to check the level of light to be used backstage during rehearsals and performances. These are usually blue lamps, which will not show up if they spill slightly onto stage, but will give sufficient light for people to see their way around in the wings.

- check it with other lanterns, if it is intended that it work with them, for example in producing a general cover of light across the stage;
- finally be sure that every knob, lever and wing nut is locked off tight, so that, now it is focused, the lantern does not move.

There are likely to be a minimum of three electrics staff plus the lighting designer involved in focusing, one to actually focus and two to look after the access equipment (although this can be done by stage staff as well) and to bring up each circuit on the board. This is usually done by using a remote control from the lighting board, which enables channels to be called up from anywhere in the theatre. Usually battery powered, and sometimes with an infrared (cordless) connection, this device is usually called the 'rigger's remote'.

Focusing will take many hours, though exactly how long depends on the size of the rig, the complexity of what each lantern has to do, the ease of access to each unit, how much scenery has to be in place to focus each lantern, whether there are delays because of faults with equipment and, most importantly, the skill of the lighting designer and LX crew. Experienced electricians will probably take an average of two minutes to focus each lantern that is easy to reach and is doing a straightforward job, and five minutes if it is difficult to reach or doing a very specific job.

During focusing is a good opportunity for the production manager to catch up with paperwork and other jobs, with the occasional visit to the stage to see how things are going, particularly when breaks are due.

LIGHTING

The beginning of lighting is an important part of any production, and the production manager will want to make sure that everyone is ready for it to start, that the first scene is set up, and that the stage is looking tidy. It is likely to be the first time that the director and designer have seen the set on stage. Although they will be familiar with the model, will have had a mark-up in rehearsal and probably seen the set being built and painted, the reality of it on stage is often a surprise to some creative teams, particularly in terms of size and the practicalities of how a set actually works. The production manager must be available to answer any queries, demonstrate how things work and make notes of any jobs that need doing.

The chart at the beginning of Chapter 4 shows who else should be at lighting sessions. It is obvious that the lighting designer needs to

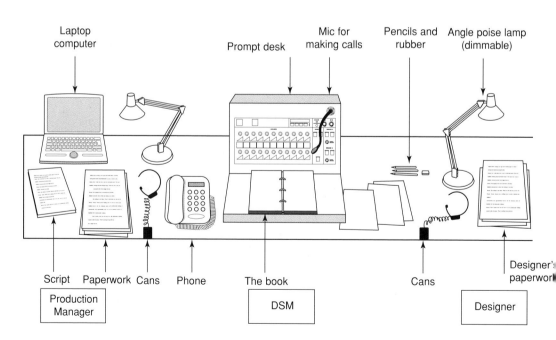

The layout of a production desk.

be there, but it is equally vital that the director and designer attend. The DSM will join them at the production desk with the book and all their paperwork.

Stage management should be available to 'walk for lighting' – to recreate the moves the actors make during the show – and move furniture and props, and stage crew should be available to move scenery. As well as the lighting board operator, at least one electrician should be available to fault find and to do some refocusing if necessary.

As it involves working through the show scene by scene, the lighting session is a good opportunity to go through scene changes to see if the intended plot will actually work. Staff will not be needed to do things the whole time, and so lighting can easily be seen as dead time; but the production manager should encourage all departments to make good use of the time – producing lists for them if necessary. It is a

good opportunity for stage management to start setting up the wings and laying out prop tables, for the crew to make sure all the backstage area is tidy, and for sound to install and check communication equipment (cans, cue lights and video monitors). It can also be a good time to set out the orchestra pit, if appropriate; though again, everyone should remember the need for quiet to allow for concentration and easy communication.

The lighting designer should have found time to put some basic building blocks, known as groups, into the lighting board. This will put together individual lanterns that are intended to be used together, for example general cover, backlight, sidelight, and lights intended for the cyc, or backcloth, in different colours, so that one instruction brings on a number of circuits.

It is a good idea for the lighting session to start with a tour of the board. This allows the lighting designer to show the director and set

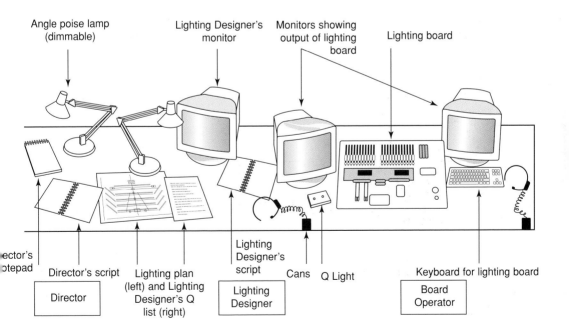

Angle poise lamp (dimmable) | Lighting Designer's monitor | Monitors showing output of lighting board | Lighting board

Director's notepad | Director's script | Lighting plan (left) and Lighting Designer's Q list (right) | Lighting Designer's script | Cans | Q Light | Keyboard for lighting board

Director | Lighting Designer | Board Operator

Plotting the Preset

The preset is the lighting state that the audience sees when they enter the auditorium. A lot of directors and lighting designers spend a long time creating this state at the beginning of a lighting session. This is not necessarily a productive use of time: it may be better to start lighting the actual scenes of the play, and then consider the preset once a feel for the lighting has been established and everyone is more familiar with the rig and what it can do.

designer what is available in the pallet of light they have designed and focused, before starting to actually light the show. As well as general colours and directions, lanterns with specific functions (specials) can be demonstrated.

The lighting designer will start to create the first lighting state by calling out levels of intensity for circuit numbers or groups, which the lighting board operator will bring up on the lighting board, and which will appear on stage. Once the creative team are happy with the look of the first lighting state, stage management will be asked to walk to different parts of the stage to ensure that an actor standing there would be adequately lit. The lighting designer may make minor adjust-

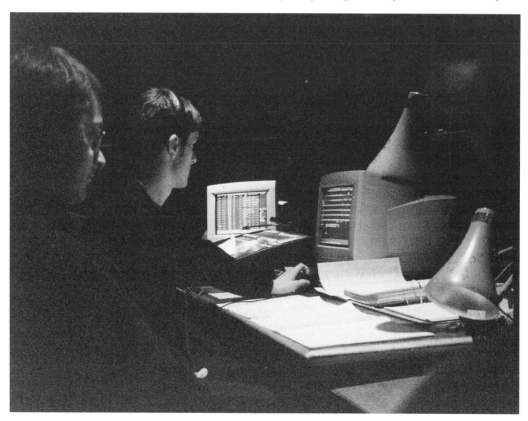

Plotting during a lighting session.

ments, and will then ask for the lighting state to be plotted – that is, recorded by the lighting board using the same memory number as cue number. At this point, a time will be given to the lighting cue. This determines how long it takes for the lighting state to establish, and how long it takes for the previous state to fade out. The position of the cue in the book will be confirmed with the DSM who will also note the time of the cue and roughly what it does.

GOING INTO SHADOWS		LX Q List version 2				5th August
Q Number	Time (Sec)	Act/Scene	Page	Action		Notes
LX Q 0.5		1/1	0	Preset – dressing on gauze		
LX Q 1		1/1	0	DBO – IN PIT		
LX Q 2		1/1	0	Build pit.		When complete, Q conductor
LX Q 3	10	1/1	3	Build light over table		
LX Q 4	10	1/1	3	Build room & table		With fly Q 1 (gauze out)
LX Q 5	10	1/2	4	Build Tarik entrance (SL)		
LX Q 6	10	1/2	5	Visual – Loose SL under screen as T. moves DS		
LX Q 7	10	1/2	11	Build CS and trolley		
LX Q 8	15	1/3	13	Build scene change state		
LX Q 9	20	1/3	14	X fade – counter top		With video Q2
LX Q 10	Snap	1/4	15	Build chorus behind counter		
LX Q 11	20	1/4	21	Build DS, backlight on table, loose US of counter, build quartet		
LX Q 12	15	1/4	21	Build SR area for chorus loose DS		
LX Q 13	15	1/4	25	Build table, loose SR area, build chorus behind counter (low level)		
LX Q 14	10	1/4	35	X fade – backlight on table, build chorus behind counter		With video Q5
LX Q 15 and f/o	10	1/4	41	Build table, loose chorus. f/o – loose string quartet		
LX Q 16 and f/o	10	1/4	43	Build chorus SR. f/o – table in backlight		
LX Q 17	15	1/4	47	Build string quartet		
LX Q 18	10	1/4	50	Build table and table area		
LX Q 19	20	1/4	54	Focus chorus and table DS of bar (low level)		
LX Q 20	15 up 60 dn	1/4	57	Build DSC for ensemble, loose table		
LX Q 21	15	1/4	62	Build chorus DS of bar		
LX Q 22	10	1/4	65	Build table		
LX Q 22.5	5	1/4	66	Build JJ for relay		
LX Q 23	10	1/4	68	Build DS area for chorus		
LX Q 24	10	1/4	71	Loose DS area		
LX Q 25	10	1/4	73	Build DS area for chorus		
LX Q 26	10	1/4	78	X fade to JJ only		With video Q 6
LX Q 27	3	1/4	78	B/O		With video Q 7
LX Q 28	10	1/5	79	Build scene change state		

An example of a lighting Q list.

Production Desk

This is a table or series of tables that will be set up in the auditorium for the duration of the production week (see pages 156-57). On it will be:

- A monitor showing the output of the lighting board, if not the lighting board itself.
- The lighting plan, and all the lighting designer's other paperwork, lit by a dim light.
- A space for the director and designer, again with suitable light. The director should be able to get out easily in order to get on stage and talk to the actors.
- A space for the DSM, ideally with the prompt desk itself. Having the prompt desk here saves a lot of time during the technical rehearsal, and it can be moved to its show position for dress rehearsals.
- A space for the production manager at one end so that they can get out easily to deal with any technical moments; also their laptop if appropriate, and all their paperwork.
- A phone to keep in touch with the rest of the building and the outside world.
- Cans for the DSM, production manager, board operator, lighting designer and, if they wish, director.

The lighting designer will then move on to the next lighting state, working from the cue list they have produced in conjunction with the director and DSM, and either modify the lighting state which is on stage to form a new state, or start again from a blackout.

Lighting a show is a long process. With an experienced lighting designer and board operator working from a well planned and agreed cue list, forty cues might be plotted per four-hour session.

The production manager may want to spend quite a lot of the lighting session with the creative team at the production desk. It is not only lighting issues that will come up at this stage, and it is useful to be there to sort out problems, answer queries and update the jobs list. Other departments should be scheduled to come on stage and start on jobs in the breaks between lighting sessions, to ensure that as much as possible is ready for the technical rehearsal.

OTHER PREPARATIONS

It is vital that everything possible has been looked at, listened to, tried, tested and agreed with the relevant members of the creative team before the technical rehearsal begins. The phrase 'We'll work that out at the tech' should ring alarm bells for production managers. The tech should be about making sure that all the plotted and rehearsed elements of the production work together as planned. It is not the time to start creating things from scratch, re-thinking the blocking or discussing the actors' motivation!

The sound designer should have played all the music and sound effects to the director before the show moves into the theatre, but they will need a plotting session now that the set is on stage. Sitting in the auditorium with the director, the sound designer will have the operator play each sound effect or piece of music. They will decide, in conjunction with the director, which speakers to use, the volume of each sound (known as the level), whether it needs any effects such as reverberation or delay, and whether the tone of the sound needs altering. At the sound plotting session they will work through the show and make these decisions for each sound cue. They will also confirm cue points with the DSM, and make sure the sound operator plots all the information and is happy with how to operate the show. Absolute quiet is needed for the sound plotting session, and the production manager should ensure that this is achieved. The only other work that can be successfully scheduled alongside sound plotting is a paint call.

Depending on the nature of the production, other pre-tech events could include scene change rehearsals, a costume parade under lights on stage, and a fight rehearsal. For operas, there will be at least one *sitzprobe*, where the orchestra are in the pit for the first time and the singers sit on stage and sing their part. In a musical, this will also include balancing orchestral and radio mics.

It is a good idea for stage management to have a props parade with the director and designer a few days before the technical rehearsal. This involves setting up all the props, perhaps in the rehearsal room, so that they can be agreed and any problems sorted out before they arrive on stage at the technical rehearsal.

THE TECHNICAL REHEARSAL

The technical rehearsal is the period when all aspects of the production are put together on stage for the first time. Everyone involved in the production has a job to do at the tech, and every moment of the show is worked through in sequence. The rehearsal does not move on to the next moment until every aspect is right. It is the key point of every production, and the most stressful. Time pressures are beginning to mount as the first night approaches, and everyone is likely to be fairly tense.

The production manager should take an active part in keeping things relaxed, but also in keeping the tech moving forwards. They should have discussed in advance with the director and stage manager how best to run the tech. Some directors like to be on cans and to take a very active part in all aspects of the tech; others prefer to leave the detailed organization of it to production management, and to concentrate on what they see and hear hap-

pening, and on what the actors are doing. One method of working is for the production manager to be on cans at the production desk with the director close by, and for the stage manager to be in the front row, again on cans so that they can stop and start the action and keep the company informed about what is happening. The following two pages show everyone's responsibilities during this crucial part of making shows happen.

The acting company will be given a half-hour call to be ready for the start of the technical rehearsal, during which time they should be getting into costume. They should be called to the stage by the DSM thirty minutes later. The director may want to say a few words about how they intend to conduct the

---

A Smooth Tech

It is vital to the smooth running of a tech that:
- everything has been worked out in advance;
- lighting and sound cues have been plotted, and scene changes rehearsed;
- there are good setting lists from the DSM in rehearsals, and everything is preset in the right place for the top of the show, and has been shout-checked;
- everyone is ready to start on time;
- all equipment, particularly cans and cue lights, is working correctly and has been tested;
- all operators are familiar with how to use equipment, and have received their cue sheets in advance;
- all technical actions have a cue number so they can easily be identified if they need changing, or as a reference point;
- all health and safety matters have been addressed in advance so that the rehearsal can progress safely.

EVERYONE'S ROLE AT THE TECH	
Director	In overall charge of the rehearsal. Making sure that their vision of how the production will work is being achieved. Adjusting what has been plotted or rehearsed, especially cue points, times and sequences, with the lighting designer, sound designer and DSM. Adjusting what has been rehearsed with the performers, choreographer and musical director. Giving notes to stage management, crew and other technicians via the production manager or stage manager. Discussing how aspects of the production look and work with the set and costume designers.
Set designer	Making sure everything looks and works as intended and giving notes via production management.
Costume designer	Making sure all costumes look and fit as intended and giving notes via the wardrobe supervisor. Reassuring the company that they look good. Giving any notes about wigs and make-up either to specialists or to the performers.
Lighting designer	Adjusting lighting states and times with the board operator. Adjusting cue points with the DSM. Giving instruction to followspot operators.
Sound designer	Adjusting sound levels with the sound operator. Adjusting cue points with the DSM.
Musical director	Conducting musical numbers. Playing the piano if appropriate (the band are unlikely to be at the tech). Taking notes about the music from the director. Working with the sound designer and operator on sound levels, particularly foldback (the amount of sound being heard in the orchestra pit or off-stage). Working with the stage manager on the best place to restart from each time the tech is stopped during musical numbers.
Stage manager	Stopping and starting the rehearsal as required by the director. Keeping the company informed about why the rehearsal has stopped and what is the reason for any delay. Supervising their team and the crew in carrying out scene changes. Updating setting list and keeping all plots up to date. Taking notes about any alterations needed to props.
DSM	Cueing the show for the first time. Adjusting cue points in the book with the director, lighting and sound designers. Communicating with the stage manager about where to set back to and when to restart the rehearsal.
ASM	Making sure props are set where needed by the performers, changing setting lists as needed. Carrying out their cues.
Technical manager	Making sure that all aspects of the set and scene changes are working properly. Taking notes of jobs that need doing to improve these. Carrying out cues if they will be working the show.

EVERYONE'S ROLE AT THE TECH (continued)	
Stage crew and Flys	Carrying out cues as directed by the DSM. Altering plots. Carrying out notes in breaks between cues if appropriate.
Construction	HOD attending the tech for important moments such as major scene changes. HOD getting notes from designer and production manager and making their own. Rest of department in workshop completing unfinished items, clearing up or preparing for next work session on stage.
Paintshop	Visiting the tech from time to time to see how the set looks under light. Getting notes from designer and production manager and making their own. In paintshop completing unfinished items, clearing up or preparing for next work session on stage.
Props	HOD attending the tech for important moments such as first use of major props. HOD getting notes from designer and production manager and making their own. Rest of department in workshop completing unfinished items, clearing up or preparing for next work session on stage. Liaising with stage management over props notes which are coming up, including work on props which stage management originally acquired.
Wardrobe supervisor	In the auditorium as much as possible. Taking notes from the costume designer, making their own and communicating those notes to the rest of the department. Overseeing quick changes, particularly from the point of view of making them easier.
Dressers	In dressing rooms or the wings carrying out quick changes and helping the company into and out of costumes. Moving costumes to where they are needed the next time.
Electrics	One member operating the lighting board. Others operating followspots or carrying out cues on stage. Others available to fault find, refocus and take notes.
Sound	One member operating the sound desk. Others available to fault find and carry out notes if appropriate.
Performers	Acting their parts as rehearsed. If necessary, staying in position when the action is stopped so that they can be lit. Being aware of what else is happening on stage and if necessary adjusting what they do to fit in with this. Not leaving the stage area until they have been told by stage management that they will not be going back over a scene. Using entrances and exits, props and costumes, probably for the first time. Liaising with stage management over problems with props. Liaising with the costume designer and wardrobe over costume problems. Trying not to get bored during long sessions when others are working very hard but they themselves have little to do.

A DSM at the prompt desk during a tech.

tech, and should then hand over to the stage manager for introductions and a safety briefing. Everyone working on the show should be introduced to the company, and the stage manager should then address any safety issues from the risk assessment. They should then take the company on a tour of the set, both onstage and offstage, pointing out any hazards, entrances and exits, the location of props tables and quick-change areas, and anything else the company needs to know about.

The stage manager should then tell the creative team that they are ready to start, ask company to stand by for the top of the show, and make sure that everything is set for the opening of the show. The DSM will ask for the

LX and sound presets, put all relevant operators on standby and, after taking a deep breath, try and cue the opening sequence of the show. It is unusual to get very far through this before the director stops the action, but if possible it is a good idea to try and run the sequence unless there is any danger, or things go hopelessly wrong. It is worth remembering at this point that, while the company have had three weeks or more of rehearsals, this is the DSM's first chance to rehearse their part in the show, and they will be under tremendous pressure to get things right quickly.

An efficient system needs establishing for stopping the rehearsal. The best is for the director to ask for this to happen, and the production manager to announce on cans the need to stop. The stage manager, in the front of the auditorium, will convey this to the performers and musical director. Although it is most often done by the director, anyone – production manager, stage management, designers, performers, crew – should stop the tech if they believe there is any danger involved.

Once the tech has stopped, the reason needs ascertaining and director, lighting designer, production manager and DSM will go to work in sorting out the problem. The stage manager should inform the company of why things were stopped, and as soon as the information is available from the director via the DSM, state the line or action they will be going back to. Getting this information early saves time, as stage management, wardrobe and crew can be setting back. However, nothing should be moved until it is clear that it is not needed for lighting. It may also be important that the company stay in place so they can be lit, and the stage manager should make sure they keep quiet so that concentration is not lost, and those who need to, can communicate about sorting out the problem.

The production manager can help the DSM, particularly in running busy sequences where

Taking notes during a tech.

they may not have the time to write down notes about cueing given by the director or lighting designer. The production manager should ask for a photocopy of the prompt script once the lighting and sound sessions have been completed. In this way they will not only have the cues marked, but also all the cuts and changes to text, as the DSM will have been noting these throughout rehearsals. For busy sequences, write down the cue numbers in a list and make notes of creative team comments as the DSM cues the sequence. Once the tech stops again, go through these notes with the DSM so that they can make the necessary adjustments before running it again.

Occasionally it may not be possible to sort out a problem immediately, and it may be necessary to note it and move on. However, it is important to remember to find time to tech the sequence involving the problem once it has been fixed. Do not leave it until the dress rehearsal and then attempt to run it.

It is important that everyone keeps their paperwork (setting lists, running plots and cue sheets) up to date during the tech, and also notes anything that needs sorting out. The rule is, write it down -- you will not remember it afterwards unless you have notes to refer to. It is worth the production manager checking that everyone is doing this, possibly via their HODs, especially if they have new or inexperienced staff. The DSM must be given time to

165

THE BEGGAR'S OPERA Onstage Rehearsal Schedule		
Tuesday 6 June	10.00 – 1.00 2.00 2.35 3.00 – 6.00	**Sitzprobe** including chorus Half hour call **Safety tour of the set** **Stage and piano 1**
Wednesday 7 June	9.25 10.00 – 1.00 2.00 2.15 – 5.15	Half hour call **Stage and piano 2** Cast called back **Stage and piano 3**
Thursday 8 June	9.25 10.00 – 1.00 2.15 2.30 – 5.30	Half hour call **Stage and piano 4** Cast called back **Stage and orchestra 1**
Friday 9 June	9.55 10.30 – 12.30 1.45 2.00 – 5.00	Half hour call **Stage and orchestra 2** Cast called back **Stage and orchestra 3**
Monday 12 June	9.25 10.00 – 1.00 2.25 3.00 – 6.00	Half hour call **Piano dress rehearsal 1** (1st cast) Half hour call **Piano dress rehearsal 2** (2nd cast)
Tuesday 13 June	1.25 2.00 – 6.00	Half hour call **Dress rehearsal 1** (1st cast)
Wednesday 14 June	1.25 2.00 – 6.00	Half hour call **Dress rehearsal 2** (2nd cast)
Thursday 15 June	7.00	**First performance** (1st cast)
Friday 16 June		No performance
Saturday 17 June	6.25 7.00	Half hour call **Performance** (2nd cast)

An example of an opera production schedule.

make changes to their book and operators, particularly sound, to amend their plots.

Teching a Show

In drama, the tech will continue for several sessions. A useful calculation is that it takes at least four times as long to tech a show as it does to run it, so a three-hour show would take at least twelve hours to tech, more if it is complicated technically. It is a good idea to have planned with the director how far they should aim to get during each session of the technical rehearsal.

Technical Rehearsals in Opera

Technical rehearsals happen in a different way in opera, and there is not the same pressure to get everything right before moving on. The sequence of rehearsals starts with a number of stage and piano rehearsals. As the name implies, this involves the company on stage with piano accompaniment only. The director (often called the producer in opera) will work through the show but concentrate more on the performers than the technical aspects. The lighting designer will be left to work with the DSM.

To protect voices, there are unlikely to be more than two stage and piano rehearsals in one day. After stage and pianos come stage and orchestra rehearsals. This involves working through the opera again, this time with the orchestra. The conductor makes the decisions about whether to stop and where to go back to. This will usually be for musical reasons only. The director is a little more free to look at technical aspects.

There will then be a piano dress rehearsal and a full dress rehearsal, although to protect voices and because of repertoire scheduling these may be several days apart.

The production manager should be planning in advance the best use of stage time during breaks in the technical rehearsal. Nearly all departments will want time on stage to complete jobs or make adjustments, and the production manager needs to referee the situation and decide who can have time on stage and when, based on the needs of the show. It works well to discuss the use of breaks with HODs when they visit the technical rehearsal, as they should all do from time to time.

The first session of a tech is always the slowest as people find their feet, get used to working together as a team and become familiar with the set, the equipment and how it is being used for the show. The director and lighting and sound designers may still be setting the conventions for the show, and things will speed up as everyone settles into their roles.

Pressure will mount if the end of the sessions allocated for the technical rehearsal approaches and there is still a considerable amount of the show to rehearse. A decision may have to be made to forego one of the dress rehearsals in order to complete the tech properly and safely. This needs to be balanced against how long it is since the beginning of the show was rehearsed, and whether anyone will remember what they were supposed to do. It can be a good idea to stick to the time of the first dress rehearsal, run as much as has been teched, and then continue teching afterwards. On a very complex show it can be worth allowing time at the end of each day to run what has been rehearsed that day. Stage management and wardrobe will need some time to set everything back to where it is needed for the start of that run, and time needs to be scheduled for this.

Eventually the technical rehearsal will get to the end of the show and there will be time for the company to take a break while everyone prepares for the first dress rehearsal. By this point there will be a long list of jobs that need to be done, and the production manager should prioritize these to ensure that those vital to the smooth running of the dress rehearsal do get done. It is best to try and schedule a technical work session between the end of the technical rehearsal and the first dress rehearsal. This will also give stage management and wardrobe time to get everything to where it should be for the top of the show – known as setting up.

Fights

Hopefully the only fights during the tech will be those that have been rehearsed in the rehearsal room, although artistic temperament and technical problems can lead to some very tense moments.

It is important not to rush the teching of fights. The fight director must be involved and the correct lighting states must be used as well as the actual costumes, especially footwear, and the actual weapons.

The fight should first be stepped through in working light so that everyone can get used to doing it on the set. Then it should be run at proper speed. Once this is satisfactory and safe, technical elements can be added. If there are to be gunshots or explosions, the DSM should have a backstage call in the book warning of these.

DRESS REHEARSALS

Dress rehearsals should be regarded as performances without an audience. The show should be run as intended in performance, and should only stop if there is a major problem, particularly one involving the safety of performers, stage management or technicians.

The production manager is again there to facilitate everyone's work. They should be on cans at the production desk and making their own notes of things that go wrong or need changing or re-rehearsing. They will also get notes from the director and other members of the creative team, and should volunteer to make notes for others, particularly the DSM, who may be too busy to write their own notes down.

During the dress rehearsal the production manager should make a point of spending a few minutes sitting in the front row to see what the view is like from there, particularly

The view from an end seat in the front row. Designer: Jessica Curtis.

Dress Rehearsal Notes		
Job	LX	Missing house lights
Job	Stage	Repair holes in gauze
Job	PM	Arrange auditorium cleaning
Act 1		
Note	SM	Why delay in starting after clearance?
Note	DSM	Anticipate Qs during opening sequence
Note	Flys	Fly Q1 (front gauze out) faster
Job	Flys	Check out dead on bar 6
Note	DSM	Move trap Q 2 to old position
Job	Paintshop	Timber inside trap to go black
Note	Wardrobe	Still problems with Mrs P's wig
Job	Workshop	Double door squeaking
Note	DSM	Split LX Q 15 (blackout) and Fly Q4
Job	LX	Check focus of SL projector
(these jobs noted from end seats when checking round auditorium)		
Job	Paintshop	Scaff bar and clamp at top of SR stairs (black)
Job	Paintshop	More breaking down on double doors
Job	Crew	Light leak between DSR flat and pros
Job	Crew	Check masking thru SR door
Job	LX	Haul up tripes mid SL
Job	LX	Neaten cables to auditorium boom SR
Note	SM	SR door to stay open after 'Let Us Take the Road'
Note	ASMs	Go on cans whenever free
Note	DSM	Split standbys end scene 9 into scene 10
Note	Flys	Front gauze in slower (to hit floor on last beat of music)
Note	SM	Wait longer before dropping iron for interval

An example of notes taken during a dress rehearsal.

how much activity in the wings can be seen. They might need to adjust the masking, or make people in the wings aware of when they can be seen. The production manager should also walk discretely about the auditorium, especially the ends of rows and the back row and should make notes about anything, not just on stage, that would be distracting or unacceptable to a member of the audience.

At the end of each dress rehearsal there should be two notes sessions: actors notes and technical notes. If technical notes are likely to be brief, it makes sense to have them immediately, while the actors are getting out of cos-tume. All stage management and operators should join the production manager, HODs and the creative team at the production desk with their running plots.

Either the director or production manager should run the technical notes session, which should concentrate on problems to do with running the show. With everyone there together it will be possible to find out exactly what went wrong with certain sequences and work out what to do to put them right. Many of the problems are likely to be to do with the fact that the show was being run for the first time and that people did not have as long between

Photographs

At some point during production week there will also be a photocall. This is an opportunity for press photographers to take set-up photographs of the performers on stage to accompany any reviews in their newspaper. Organized and overseen by the publicity department, it is usually best scheduled before the start of a dress rehearsal. Members of wardrobe and stage management will need to be in attendance, and there will need to be a bright lighting state. A photographer will usually be employed by the theatre or production company to take action shots during a dress rehearsal, and press photographers sometimes attend these as well. Production management need to ensure that the front row of the auditorium is clear for photographers at these times.

cues as they thought they would from timings at the technical rehearsal.

The director will want to get to notes with the actors, and the DSM should go with them once all problems to do with running the show have been discussed. The designers should remain at the notes session in the auditorium, and the production manager should go through their jobs list and add jobs from all other departments to arrive at the definitive list.

Actors notes sessions will mainly be to do with their performances, but issues may arise to do with props, costume, scenery, lighting or sound. Cue points, particularly for entrances and exits, may be altered. It is therefore essential that the DSM is at actors' notes to make these changes in the book and to feedback any problems to the production manager and relevant departments.

Separate notes sessions may be arranged between the lighting designer and DSM (to discuss cueing points) with the musical director and the band, and for any other notes that only involve one department. The final thing to do at this point is to agree the use of stage time before the next dress rehearsal. Here the production manager again needs to referee the situation and perhaps make some unpopular decisions. Because of the pressure of time, departments are unlikely to get as long on stage that they would like, and some departments may have to be asked to make early starts or late finishes in order to get their jobs complete. The production manager should try and give as much notice of these sorts of calls as possible, and still work within union and national regulations regarding hours of work and breaks.

Depending on the schedule, there may be further dress rehearsals or previews, or it may be time for the first night of the show. Production managers should try to avoid any major changes to cueing sequences, the set, masking or props between the last dress rehearsal and the first night. There is unlikely to be time to try them out, and this can lead to a disastrous or dangerous situation, due to unforeseen knock-on effects of the changes.

THE FIRST NIGHT AND BEYOND

Chapter 1 details what the production manager should do during and after the first performance, and this can be almost the end of their direct involvement with the production. While the production is running they may be working on the next show in the same theatre or another project elsewhere. It is a good idea to watch the show a few days after it has opened and, in conjunction with the director, give any technical notes that have arisen as a result of the show settling in. These are likely to be mainly to do with timing of cues.

Amateur production managers may be around for subsequent performances; professional ones are unlikely to be, and will leave the stage manager to look after the show unless there are major problems arising on the **show reports**. These are produced by the stage manager at the end of every performance, and should have input from all operators and stage management. They are distributed at the end of the show to the artistic director, director, conductor, production manager and HODs. The stage manager and DSM each keep a copy. One should also be displayed so as to be available to non-show staff the next morning in case any repairs need doing. It should be remembered that if there is an accident, the show report may be used as a piece of evidence.

First Night Superstitions

Some directors will not set the curtain call until after the final dress rehearsal, which can mean that it is under-rehearsed and goes wrong on the first night.

Some will not allow the last line of the play to be spoken before the first performance; this again can lead to cueing problems, or even to the actors forgetting what the last line actually is.

Particularly superstitious actors will not wish a fellow performer 'good luck': if they say anything it might be 'break a leg!' or 'Toi, Toi, Toi'.

The show in performance (see illustrations on pages 76, 77 and 81). Photo: Mike Rothwell

For a show report to be a useful document it should be carefully written and should contain:

- running times for each act plus the length of the interval(s);
- how many curtain calls were taken;
- the number in the audience (from the front-of-house manager);
- anything which was not 'as rehearsed' or went wrong or nearly went wrong (specifying cue numbers and what they do);
- any accident or incident (also complete an accident report sheet);
- information on what has been done, or what needs to be done, to avoid the problem occurring again;
- anything that needs maintenance or repair;
- any major problems with lines;
- any organizational problems;
- anyone who was late for the half, or beginners;
- any disturbances;
- any notes given or things changed or re-plotted after the show, including changes of timings and Q points as the show settles in;
- the effect of anything changed since the last show (e.g. Q points which worked better/worse);
- anything which has been cut.

If no problems occurred, the show report should state that it was a 'clean show'.

After a production has, opened it is a good idea for a debrief to be organised to discuss any problems and what could be done to avoid them in the future, and also what worked well. Staff should be encouraged to be as open as possible at these, but also to be positive and not just look at the bad points.

Once all invoices have been paid, a summary of expenditure against costs should be produced and discussed with HODs. Reasons for overspends should be addressed so that they can be avoided in future. Reasons for underspends should also be discussed, as it may mean that initial costings were inaccurate, which could have meant unnecessary compromises having to be made at the production meeting stage.

THE GET-OUT

The production manager's final job on a production is to arrange the get-out of the show and to return the theatre to the state it was in at the start of the production process. Details of this will depend on whether or not the show has a future life, for example a tour or a transfer. The same principles of organization, communication, planning and safety apply to closing a show as they do to making it happen in the first place.

If the show is touring or transferring, a production manager's workload can instantly be doubled. Every aspect of the production needs documenting during the run so that it can be re-created at the next theatre. Usually all the physical aspects of the show will be toured, with the exception of lighting equipment. The chart on pages 174-75 shows everyone's involvement with a show touring or transferring. The production manager will, as usual, take an overview of this, but will have additional decisions to make to do with the future life of the production.

If a show does not have a future life, the get-out and breaking up of the production needs to be organized. Discussions should be held with each department about what is to be kept. This will depend on where the items came from in the first place, the theatre's policy, and the availability of storage. The most likely items to be kept are costumes, props and furniture. All borrowed or hired items need to be returned to their owners. When goods are returned it is important that they are on time and in good condition so as to keep good will and not incur additional costs.

If items are being thrown away, rubbish skips will need to be organized. Transport to stores and hire companies will need to be arranged, and staff called for the get-out. It is here that the largest number of casuals are likely to be needed, as the work is not particularly skilled and must be finished as soon as possible.

It is as important, from both an efficiency and a safety point of view, that everyone knows what they will be doing on a get-out, what is being kept, and where everything needs to go. The production manager should draw up and publish a list of this, and go through it with resident staff at a get-out meeting during the week in which the show closes. Departments should then work in teams, probably with casuals, and report back to the production manager when tasks are complete or when they encounter problems.

The production manager should, once again, take an overview and co-ordinate everyone's work. The aim is to completely remove the production from the stage, dressing rooms and backstage areas; to put away or return all items to do with the show; and to return the theatre to the clean and tidy state it was in before the production started.

CONCLUSION

All staff, including production managers, can learn from their own experiences, and from the work of others on productions. In theatre no one ever stops learning; that is part of its attraction. This book has attempted to put together guidance from experiences that have worked and from those that have not, to give anyone wanting or having to production manage a show a foundation to work from.

Shows will still happen even with no production management, or worse, with poor production management. Staff and creative teams will look after their own interests; creativity and collaboration will be replaced by conflict and confusion. However, with efficient, organized, forward-thinking, resourceful and committed production management in place, everyone can concentrate on using their specific skills to produce enjoyable and exciting theatre.

Everyone's Responsibilities with Tours and Transfers		
	Transfer	**Tour**
Director	Visit venue during design process Possibly attend lighting session Run technical and dress rehearsals Watch the first night and give notes	Attend a dress rehearsal, if there is one, on the first date of the tour and give notes Watch the first night on tour and give notes
Set designer	Visit venue during design process Draw groundplan of set in the transfer venue Possibly attend lighting session Attend technical and dress rehearsals Watch the first night and give notes	Possibly draw groundplans for each venue on tour, more usually done by the production or company manager If free, attend dress rehearsal, if there is one, on the first date of the tour and give notes Watch the first night on tour and give notes
Costume designer	Attend technical and dress rehearsal Watch the first night and give notes	No involvement
Lighting designer	Visit venue during design process Draw lighting plan for the transfer venue Liaise with chief LX of the venue about requirements Run focusing session Run lighting session Adjust lighting during technical and dress rehearsal Watch the first night and give notes	Possibly draw lighting plans for each venue on tour, more usually done by the touring production electrician or company manager if they are responsible for re-lights Possibly re-light the show on the first date of the tour If free, attend a dress rehearsal, if there is one, on the first date of the tour
Sound designer	Liaise with venue over requirements Run plotting session Adjust sound during technical and dress rehearsal Watch the first night and give notes	Unlikely to be involved *Sound on tour is likely to be the responsibility of an ASM or dedicated sound operator. If a sound system is not toured, company or stage manager are likely to be responsible for plotting levels and resident staff for operating.*
Stage manager	*The stage manager from the originating theatre may go with the show for the full run, or may go until the show opens and then hand over to the venue's stage manager* Pack props and furniture at the end of the last performance Carry out show duties as for the run at the originating venue	*A stage manager, or company manager, is likely to be engaged for a tour. They will be in charge of all aspects of the tour. Their specific duties will include welfare and administration of the company, paying salaries and agreeing box office figures. They may also be responsible for re-lighting the show in each venue. The stage manager of the originating venue will hand the show over to them before the tour starts* Oversee the packing of the whole show at the end of each date on the tour and unpacking and setting up at each venue Carry out stage manager's show duties as for the run at the originating venue
DSM	*Almost certain to go with the show* Cueing the show as at the originating venue	*Almost certain to go with the show* Cueing the show as at the originating venue
ASM	If going with the show, helping to pack up props and furniture. If not going, send unambiguous setting and running lists for venue's ASM Setting up the show and carrying out cues as at the originating venue	*Will probably go with the show, or a touring ASM will take over the show before the tour starts* Setting up the show and carrying out cues as at the originating venue

	Transfer	Tour
Technical manager	*May go to the venue for the fit up* Responsible for dismantling and packing the set at the end of the last performance	*A touring carpenter may be engaged to go with the show or just for each fit up on tour, with the comapny manager running the get outs* *The technical manager of each venue will run the resident crew*
Stage crew and Flys	Responsible for dismantling and packing the set at the end of the last performance Passing plots on to stage management for use by the resident crew in the transfer	*Resident crew will fit up the show* *Resident crew will carry out cues as at the originating venue* *Resident crew will strike and pack the set at the end of the last performance*
Construction	Dismantle and pack the set in lorries at the end of the last performance No involvement once the show leaves the building	
Paintshop	No involvement except to prepare touch up kit in case the set gets damaged	
Props	No involvement	
Wardrobe supervisor	*May go to the venue until the show opens* Responsible for supplying all information about the costumes for the show to the venue's resident staff Responsible for overseeing and packing of all costumes at the end of the last performance	*A wardrobe supervisor may be engaged for the tour* Responsible for supplying all information about the costumes for the show to the touring staff Responsible for overseeing and packing of all costumes at the end of the last performance
Wardrobe	No involvement	
Dressers	*Resident staff will dress the show as at the originating venue* Help to pack up all costume items at the end of the last performance	*Resident dressers will work on the show in each venue* Help to pack up all costume items at the end of the last performance
Electrics	*Resident staff will rig, focus and operate the show as at the originating venue* De-rig the show at the end of the last performance and pack any LX which is being used at the transfer venue	*A production electrician may be engaged for the tour, in which case they may operate at each venue, otherwise resident staff will rig, focus and operate as at the originating venue* De-rig the show at the end of the last performance and pack any LX which is being toured
Sound	*Resident staff rig and operate sound as at the originating venue*	*Sound on tour is likely to be the responsibility of an ASM or dedicated sound operator* *If a sound system is not toured, company or stage manager are likely to be responsible for plotting levels and resident staff for operating*
Performers	Acting their parts at technical and dress rehearsals, which will mainly be for the benefit of the stage management and technical staff of the venue Acting their parts in performance as at the originating venue	Acting their parts at a dress rehearsal, if there is one, on the first date of the tour. This will mainly be for the benefit of the touring staff Adjusting their moves according to the size of stage at a 'placing call' before the first performance in each venue Acting their parts in performance as at the originating venue

Everyone's Responsibilities with Tours and Transfers (continued)

An example of a piece of dramatic theatre. Designer: Dora Schweitzer; Lighting Designer: Robin Carter. Photo: Laurence Burns

Appendix I
Codes of Practice for Theatre Access Equipment

GENIE

Activity	Using the Genie hoist
Location	Theatre
Staff allowed	Members of any department once trained:
Special notes	The genie can only be used on a flat floor There must be two people present when the Genie is being used (because in case of mains failure it can only be lowered from the ground)
Date of creation/revision of COP	7/1/2001
1. Approved Tasks	Accessing lighting and stage equipment and scenery at high levels by ONE PERSON The hoist MUST NOT be moved when elevated

2. Before Use

- visually check that all chains/cables have even tension and no slack
- visual check of mast and cage for damage
- do not use the machine if any checks are unsatisfactory
- disconnect machine from mains before adjusting or dismantling
- report any faults damage or maintenance carried out to Production Management
- assess the stage area for potential hazards e.g. unguarded edges, holes, traps, doors and surface irregularities
- position the Genie where you want to work
- ensure that the FOUR outriggers are locked into place in an X pattern
- (if working against a vertical wall which extends to the full height of the extended Genie. You can use the T formation with the top of the T against the wall. N.B. the wall must be part of the building not a piece of scenery)

- adjust the levelling jacks on the end of each outrigger until the pad is touching the ground. If possible the wheels should remain on the ground
- check that the bubble is centred in the spirit level mounted on the Genie. If not adjust the jacks so that it is. CHECK AGAIN that all four pads are on the ground
- ensure that the 'hold down' bar is in the vertical position
- use an extension cable to plug the transformer into the mains, ensuring that the movement of the hoist will not interfere with the cable
- check that the Genie is clear of hazards or obstructions
- ensure that anyone working near the Genie is wearing a Hard Hat

3. During use

- shout 'hoist moving' before each movement.
- be aware of what is above and below you when you move
- the hoist can be used to lift equipment etc but do not exceed the safe working load of 136kg or 300lb including the operator
- do not move the hoist when elevated.
- in the case of emergency or power failure, the platform can be lowered using the emergency valve on the side of the power unit (push and twist)

4. After use

- ensure feed cable is neatly coiled up and left with the genie if needed again
- ensure that the basket is left empty and that any paint/soiling is removed
- the Genie should always be left in the fully down position

5. Periodic checks to be done before each usage period

- disconnect machine from mains before adjusting or dismantling
- check tension on chains/cables. They should be even with no slack
- keep chains well lubricated
- check for pump noise, a noisy pump indicates a clogged oil inlet screen filter
- visual check on electric cable and plug
- check visible parts for correct operation and function
- check that moving parts operate freely and there are no breakages
- to avoid damage: Aluminium is a soft metal and is easily damaged by hammers crowbars etc. Also avoid exposure to dilute hydrochloric acid, potash, and similar substances which are corrosive to aluminium
- to avoid risk of electric shock do not allow fluids to come into contact with electrical components

6. Noise

- ensure that those in the immediate area can hear the Genie operator clearly and without distraction

7. Light

- ensure there is sufficient levels of light to allow safe movement.

8. P.P.E. and clothing

- ensure that anyone working near the Genie is wearing a Hard Hat
- the person in the cage must ensure that all tools etc. are either secured or on a lanyard and that nothing is left in the cage

USING THE TALLESCOPE

General Guidelines

- There are 3 Methods of using the Tallescope. You should study the 'for use when' section of the Code of Practice to decide which method is appropriate for the job you are doing
- For each method there are a number of rules which must be followed and pre-climbing checks which must be carried out

Before each fit up the following checks should be made (Production Management should designate who is responsible for this):

- All brakes working
- Wheels moving freely
- 2 Outriggers fitted and complete
- Bottom hooks working freely
- Ladder hooks working freely
- Ladder tipping freely
- No components bent or otherwise damaged
- Hauling line and bag fitted

General Rules

- Hard Hats to be used by everyone working in the vicinity of the tallescope
- No work to be carried out from on the tallescope ladder. If the tallescope is too tall use a conventional ladder or other method of access
- Never roll the tallescope over cables or airlines

- Never haul anything heavy up the tallescope; anything light should be hauled up within the wheelbase of the tallescope
- Never climb onto the handrail of the basket or use boxes or ladders to try and gain extra height
- Never leave any tools, components or paint in the tallescope basket
- Do not try to stretch the height by extending the legs. These are for levelling only
- Ensure that the scope footers can hear the directions of the person in the cage clearly and without distraction
- Ensure there is sufficient levels of light to allow safe movement and work

Raked Stages

On permanently raked stages or stages with a false rake added, method 3 must be used with the long axis of the tallescope facing up the rake and 2 legs extended to level the tallescope.
If an anti-rake is built and fixed to the rake, which effectively turns it into a flat floor, and assuming other criteria are met, methods 1 or 2 can then be used

TILTING UP OR DOWN

Manning

3 people are needed to tilt the Tallescope up or down

- One looks after the bottom of the ladder and does the actual tilting up or down
- The 2nd person holds the other end of the base of the Tallescope
- The 3rd person lifts the basket if tilting up or receives the basket if tilting down

TILTING UP

Checks Before Tilting Up

1 Tallescope is level (check the bubble on the spirit level fitted to the tallescope)
2 Leg clips locked
3 Ladder not extended
4 Sufficient overhead clearance
5 Anyone around aware you are about to tilt the tallescope

Checks After Tilting Up

1 Both bottom hooks engaged
2 Both bottom clips engaged

Now proceed with whichever method you are using

TILTING DOWN

Checks Before Tilting Down

1 All equipment, components etc. removed from basket
2 Ladder not extended
3 Area clear for ladder to tilt down
4 Anyone around aware you are about to tilt the tallescope

METHODS OF USING THE TALLESCOPE

METHOD 1 By One Person Alone

For use when:
The tallescope does not need to be moved
The tallescope is on a level floor
Both outriggers can be fixed at right angles to the tallescope, touching the floor
No lifting is required

Rules:
BRAKES to be ON
HARD HAT to be worn by anyone working in the vicinity
ANOTHER PERSON to be within earshot of the area being worked in
A SECOND PERSON to stay at the bottom of the tallescope if other work is going on around the area of the tallescope

Pre-climbing checks

1 Bottom hooks secure
2 Ladder at correct height and ladder hooks secure
3 Brakes ON
4 Outriggers at right angles and touching floor
5 Enough light to work safely
6 Hard hats ON

METHOD 2 Moving

For use when:
Tallescope needs to be moved
The tallescope is on a level floor
2 authorised people are available to man the bottom of the tallescope
Both outriggers can be fixed at right angles to the tallescope
The tallescope can face the direction it needs to move (along the long axis)
No lifting is required

Note

Moving the tallescope with a person up it is in contravention of the manufacturer's instructions. However, in some theatre situations, risk assessments and accident statistics show that it is safer for the tallescope to be moved with some one up it than for that person to climb the tallescope many times during a work session.

Production management should only allow the tallescope to be used in this way if they, the theatre management and licensing authorities are happy with this assessment.

Rules:

BRAKES to be OFF

HARD HATS to be worn by the 2 people manning the bottom of the tallescope and anyone working in the area

One PERSON at bottom of tallescope to be designated as IN CHARGE of the procedure

BOTH people to stay HOLDING the ends of the tallescope and CONCENTRATING on the job

Pre-climbing checks:

1 Bottom hooks secure
2 Ladder at correct height and ladder hooks secure
3 Brakes OFF
4 Outriggers at right angles and just off the floor
5 Hard hats ON

Moving:

1 Person at top says how far they wish to be moved and in which direction
2 Person in charge checks there is enough light to see to move safely
3 Person in charge checks the floor the tallescope will move over is safe, level and clear of obstructions
4 Person in charge says 'moving you'
5 Person at the top replies 'OK' if ready
6 Both people at the bottom move the tallescope
7 Person at the top says STOP when in the right place or nearing an obstruction

METHOD 3 Difficult Situations

For use when: The tallescope is not on level floor
Both outriggers cannot be fixed at right angles to the tallescope
Extra weight is going to be taken by the person at the top of the tallescope

Rules: 2 PEOPLE needed at the bottom of the tallescope
A THIRD PERSON to hold the tallescope at the side of the ladder whenever ONE outrigger cannot be used
A FOURTH PERSON to hold the tallescope at the side of the ladder if NEITHER outrigger can be used
BRAKES to be ON
HARD HATS to be worn by ALL people at the bottom of the tallescope and anyone working in the area
ONE PERSON at bottom of tallescope to be designated as IN CHARGE of the procedure
ALL people to stay HOLDING the bottom of the tallescope and CON-CENTRATING on the job
Tallescope only to be moved once person at top has come down

Pre-climbing checks:

1 Bottom hooks secure
2 Ladder at correct height and ladder hooks secure
3 If legs have been adjusted, check that the bubble is within the circle on the spirit level which is at the bottom of the ladder
4 All 4 wheels touching the floor (this may involve extending one or more leg)
5 Brakes ON
6 Outriggers as close to right angles as possible
7 Enough light to work safely
8 Hard hats ON

APPENDIX II
HEALTH AND SAFETY LEGISLATION

IN THE UK

The Health and Safety at Work Act 1974:
This is the major piece of legislation dealing with health and safety. It is an enabling act under which various regulations can be made on more specific issues.

Management of Health and Safety at Work Regulations 1992:
Require employers to carry out risk assessments, make arrangements to implement necessary measures, appoint competent people and arrange for appropriate information and training.

Workplace (Health, Safety and Welfare) Regulations 1992:
Cover a wide range of basic health, safety and welfare issues such as ventilation, heating, lighting, workstations, seating and welfare facilities.

Health and Safety (Display Screen Equipment) Regulations 1992:
Set out requirements for work with visual display units (VDUs).

Personal Protective Equipment (PPE) Regulations 1992:
Require employers to provide appropriate protective clothing and equipment for their employees.

Provision and Use of Work Equipment Regulations (PUWER) 1998:
Require that equipment provided for use at work, including machinery, is safe.

Manual Handling Operations Regulations 1992:
Cover the moving of objects by hand or bodily force.

Health and Safety (First Aid) Regulations 1981:
Cover requirements for first aid.

The Health and Safety Information for Employees Regulations 1989:
Require employers to display a poster telling employees what they need to know about health and safety.

Employers' Liability (Compulsory Insurance) Regulations 1969:
Require employers to take out insurance against accidents and ill health to their employees.

Reporting of Injuries, Diseases and Dangerous Occurrences Regulations 1995 (RIDDOR):
Require employers to notify certain occupational injuries, diseases and dangerous events.

Noise at Work Regulations 1989:
Require employers to take action to protect employees from hearing damage.

Electricity at Work Regulations 1989:
Require people in control of electrical systems to ensure they are safe to use and maintained in a safe condition.

Control of Substances Hazardous to Health Regulations 1999 (COSHH):
Require employers to assess the risks from hazardous substances and take appropriate precautions.

Chemicals (Hazard Information and Packaging for Supply) Regulations (CHIP 2) 1994:
Require suppliers to classify, label and package dangerous chemicals and provide safety data sheets for them.

Construction (Design and Management) Regulations 1994:
Cover safe systems of work on construction sites.

Gas Safety (Installation and Use) Regulations 1998:
Cover safe installation, maintenance and use of gas systems and appliances in domestic and commercial premises.

Working Time Regulations (The European Working Time Directive) 1998:
Require employers to: limit the average hours a week that a worker can be required to work to forty-eight (though workers can choose to opt out if they want to); give employees eleven hours rest a day, an in-work rest break if the working day is longer than six hours, and a day off each week; four weeks paid leave per year (pro rata).

Health and Safety (Safety Signs and Signals) Regulations 1996:
Require employers to provide specific safety signs whenever there is a risk that has not been avoided or controlled by other means.

Lifting Operations and Lifting Equipment Regulations 1998 (LOLER):
Require that lifting equipment is strong and stable enough for the particular use, and marked with a safe working load; installed and used safely; subject to on-going examination.

The Health and Safety Executive publish many guides and leaflets about the regulations and how to interpret them. Production managers should acquire as many of these as possible. Many are available from the HSE website (www.hse.gov.uk).

IN THE US

The Occupational Safety and Health Act 1970 (OSHA) requires employers to:

- Provide workplaces free from recognized hazards and comply with standards, rules and regulations issued under the Act.
- Examine workplace conditions to make sure they conform to applicable OSHA standards.
- Minimize or reduce hazards.
- Make sure employees have and use safe tools and equipment and properly maintain this equipment.
- Use colour codes, posters, labels or signs to warn employees of potential hazards.
- Establish or update operating procedures, and communicate them so that employees follow safety and health requirements.
- Provide medical examinations and training when required by OSHA standards.
- Report to the nearest OSHA office within eight hours any fatal accident, or one that results in the hospitalization of three or more employees.

In Australia

Health and Safety is regulated by the National Occupational Health and Safety Commission. Each state and territory has responsibility for making laws about workplace health and safety, and for enforcing those laws.

The Occupational Health and Safety (OHS) Act gives broad duties to the workplace parties to:

- occupational health and safety in the workplace;
- provide systems of work that are safe and without risk to health;
- prevent industrial injuries and diseases;
- protect the health and safety of the public in relation to work activities;
- rehabilitate injured workers.

Specific regulations support the principal Act by providing more detailed requirements for specific hazards. Regulations are legally binding and enforceable.

Codes of practice are issued by Commonwealth, state and territory governments to advise on acceptable ways of complying with their occupational health and safety legislation.

Duty of care requires everything 'reasonably practicable' to be done to protect the health and safety of others at the workplace. This duty is placed on:

- all employers;
- their employees; and
- any others who have an influence on the hazards in a workplace.

The latter includes contractors and those who design, manufacture, import, supply or install plant, equipment or materials used in the workplace.

Specific rights and duties logically flow from the duty of care. These include:

- provision and maintenance of safe plant and systems of work;
- safe systems of work in connection with plant and substances;
- a safe working environment and adequate welfare facilities;
- information and instruction on workplace hazards, and supervision of employees in safe work;
- monitoring the health of their employees and related records keeping;
- employment of qualified persons to provide health and safety advice;
- nomination of a senior employer representative; and
- monitoring conditions at any workplace under their control and management.

There are National Standards for manual handling, occupational noise, plant and mobile equipment, hazardous substances and dangerous goods.

It is important for production managers to find out the specific legislation for each state or territory and understand how it affects their work.

Combining the work of several departments in an opera. Photo: Laurence Burns

GLOSSARY

Acknowledgement – confirmation that an operator is standing by for a Q.
– official thanks in a programme for assistance with a production.
An **Adapter** – the person who modifies a piece of writing from one genre to another.
– a connector for changing from one type of plug or socket to another.
An **Angel** – someone who invests money in a production for a share of the profits.
Angle – the angle at which a light beam hits the stage, an actor, or piece of scenery.
An **Area** – a subdivision of the acting area for lighting design purposes so that they can be lit separately.
An **Aria** – a solo song in an opera.
A **Backing** – a musical accompaniment.
– a piece of scenery behind an opening, a door or a window to indicate the scene beyond.
– financial support for a production or company.
A **Bar** – a horizontal flown or hung pipe, usually metal on which scenery, lighting and other equipment can be suspended.
A **Barre** – a horizontal rail (either fixed to a wall or free standing) used by dancers for support when exercising.
A **Baton** – white stick with which a conductor controls and cues an orchestra and singers.
A **Batten** – a number of floodlights fixed together as a single unit.
– a length of timber (usually 3in x 1in) used to build and reinforce scenery.
Beginners – everyone who is on stage at or near the start of a show or act.
– the time and the backstage call made five minutes before the start of a show or act summoning beginners to the stage.
A **Black** – a serge or velour drape or flat usually used as masking.
Black – a lighting state without light.
Blacks – black clothing worn by Stage Management and Technicians during performances.
To **Bleed** – to emit a low level of light, either because a circuit is plotted at a low level or because of badly trimmed dimmers.
– when an unwanted colour shows through another layer of paint.
To **Bleed Through** – to increase the level of light behind a gauze so that what is behind the gauze becomes visible.
A **Block** – For rehearsal purposes, a sub–division of the play (decided by the Director), usually smaller than a scene.
– a frame in which one or more pulley wheel is mounted.
To **Block** – to plan (and, for the DSM, to write down) the actors' moves in rehearsals.
The **Board** – the control board (lighting board or sound mixer).
– the overall governing body of a theatre.
The **Boards** – the stage itself.
The **Book** – the specially prepared copy of the script from which the show is run. It contains all the moves and cues.
– the plot and dialogue of a musical.
To **Book** – to fold hinged flats together.
– to secure tickets for a performance or the services of a performer or a whole production.
A **Breakdown** – a detailed list of requirements or involvement.
To **Breakdown** – to make a costume, prop or scenic element seem dirty, worn or old.
A **Bridge** – a musical link between two more important pieces.
– a gallery above the stage or auditorium used for access and as a rigging position.
– an elevator which raises and lowers sections of the stage floor.
The **Build** – the time during which elements of a production are manufactured.
To **Build** – to increase in level.
– to construct a set from its component parts, particularly on stage as part of the fit up.
To **Build Up** – to increase an actor's part to more than is in the original script.
– to raise the level of part of a stage usually using rostra.

The **Business** – the theatre industry.

Business – bookings or takings for a production.

– action performed by an actor during a performance.

A **Cable** – a wire which can take electricity or sound feeds.

– steel rope used for flying or suspension purposes.

A **Call** – a tannoy announcement made by the person on the book either backstage or front of house.

– a working session. This can also be department specific as in wardrobe call, dance call, fight call, photocall etc.

The **Call** – the curtain call. Acknowledgement to/from the audience at the end of the performance and the moves and Qs associated with it.

– the time an Actor, Stage Manager or Technician is required for the next rehearsal or performance

To **Call** – to summon someone via the tannoy.

– to summon someone for a rehearsal or performance.

To **Call A Show** – to run a show from the Prompt Copy by giving (calling) the technical Qs.

Clearance – the message from front of house that a performance or act can be started (because all the audience are in).

– the distance between one flying piece and another.

A **Company Call** – a working session (or notification) involving all the performers.

– a curtain call involving all the performers together.

To **Cover** – to understudy a part in an opera.

– to fix material or timber to the framework of a flat or other scenic element.

The **Curtain Line** – the end of the last speech of a play.

– the position on stage where the house tabs land.

To **Cut** – to miss out lines or part of the play by mistake.

– to snap to a lighting state, even if that is not the recorded time of the Q.

– to cut cloth or patterns to make costumes.

– to decide not to have something in a production, either physical items or lines from the script.

To **Cut to** – to go to a point later in the play or opera (to save time during rehearsals).

The **Cuts** – the lines it has been decided (usually by the Director) to remove from a script.

A **Dead** – a position for a piece of scenery or furniture on stage and the mark which indicates that position.

– to set and mark the position of a piece of scenery, furniture of flying bar.

Dead – something is dead if it is no longer needed for a show. Usually refers to scenery or props.

A **Desk** – a music stand at which one or more musicians playing the same instrument sit.

The **Desk** – the lighting board or sound mixer.

– the prompt desk, where the DSM sits and operates Q lights, tannoy, etc.

– the table in the auditorium at which the creative team sit during technical and dress rehearsals.

To **Dress** – to put items which make the set look realistic and lived–in onto the set.

– to neaten, particularly a set of tabs or legs.

– to aid an actor in putting on their costume or accessories.

– to have a Dress rehearsal.

To **Lay off** – to terminate someone's employment.

– to store (usually a flat) somewhere away from its correct position on stage.

A **Lead** – a cable.

– (pronounced 'led') an extra heavy counterweight.

– a principal actor.

A **Line** – a piece of the text of a play.

– a single rope.

– a flying bar.

Line – the word called out by an actor when they need a prompt.

A **Line Run** – a run through without props, moves or action to check that everyone knows their lines.

Maintenance – the repair or checking that equipment or plant is working properly.

– the daily washing, ironing and repair of items of costume.

A **Mark** – a piece of tape or painted line on the stage floor or in the rehearsal room to show the position of a piece of scenery, furniture or an actor.

To **Mark** – to rehearse or perform without acting, dancing or singing at normal performance level.

To **Mark Out** – to put the limits of the stage and set on the floor of a rehearsal room using coloured tape, with measurements taken form the groundplan.

To **Mark Up** – to put Qs into a prompt script.

A **Mask** – a piece of metal with a fixed shaped aperture which restricts the shape of light coming from a profile lantern.

– a protective device worn over the nose and mouth to protect you from dust, fumes etc.

– a covering for the face of a performer to suggest character, wounds etc.

To **Mask** – to be in a position so that an actor or prop cannot be seen (either on purpose or by mistake).

– to position masking so that the audience cannot see into the wings or grid.

Masking – scenery, usually stock, usually black, positioned to stop the audience seeing into the wings or grid.

– the act of stopping something being seen.

The **Notice** – the announcement of the date that the run of a show is going to end.

The **Notices** – reviews of the production.

A **Pack** – a radio mic transmitter.

– a number of flats stored together against a wall or specially constructed frame work (a packing rail).

A **Plot** – a list of actions undertaken by a technician during a show.

The **Plot** – the story in a play or Opera.

To **Plot** – to record, on computer or in written form.

The **Principal Boy** – the hero in a pantomime, usually played by a female.

The **Principal Girl** – the heroine in a pantomime, always played by a female.

A **Q** – an action carried out by a technical department or Stage Management.

– a lighting state.

To **Q** – to give an instruction to carry out an action during a rehearsal or performance.

A **Q Point** – the point at which a Q is given.

A **Q Sheet** – a list of Qs that one person or department carries out.

A **Q Synopsis** – a list of what each lighting state aims to achieve.

A **Q to Q** – a rehearsal which just deals with the technical moments of a production.

A **Run** – a rehearsal of a show done without stopping.

– a number of performances at one venue.

– a number of flats fixed together in a line.

The **Run** – the performances of one production

To **Run** – to rehearse without stopping.

To **Run a flat** – to move a flat while it is in a vertical position.

A **Schedule** – a list of equipment needed for a particular job or production.

The **Schedule** – a list of all the work to be done and rehearsals for a production together with the time allocated for them.

To **Schedule** – to plan (and publish) the use of time in a production.

A **Set** – the scenery making up a scene. The set is the one for your specific show.

– a flying bar (counterweight or hemp set).

To **Set** – to position on stage.

Set – ready.

To **Set Back** – to return to a particular point in the piece. Often the beginning of an act, scene or specific sequence.

To **Set Up** – to get ready for a rehearsal or performance.

A **Standby** – the instruction to an operator or performer to be ready for an imminent Q (and its place in the prompt copy).

– a prop used if the actual fails or is damaged.

To **Walk** – at a lighting session, to move around the stage so that the lighting designer or director can check that actors will be lit in the state being plotted. Usually done by an ASM.

To **Walk Up** – to stand a piece of scenery up by pushing it up from underneath hand over hand.

The **Walkdown** – the final scene of a Pantomime in which the artists acknowledge their applause, usually wearing costumes designed just for that scene.

INDEX

Access equipment 57, 177-83
Accident Reporting 104
Acting Company 69
Amateur Stage Management 40
Amateur theatre 10, 43, 64,
    70, 71, 90, 105, 110,
    117, 120, 125, 143,
    171
Anti-rake 95
Artistic director 18
ASM (Assistant Stage Manager)
    36-7, 39, 120
Audience 7
Blacks 34
Blocking 113
Board of Directors 16
Book, the 34-5, 116-17, 159, 165
Brailing 149, 154
Budget, cuts 85
Budgeting 67-70
Build and Paint Schedule 131-3
Business plan 14
Call, half hour 161
Call, rehearsal 117-18
Casuals 40, 49, 58
Chief Electrician 58-9
Chief Executive 17
Choreographer 26
Code of practice 91, 102-4,
    177-83
Companies, Producing 11
Construction Manager 44-9
Contact details 75
Contingency 83
Contracts 22, 26, 41
Copyright 112
Costing 81-3

Costume *See* Wardrobe
Costume Designer 21-2, 111
Costume fittings 64, 120
Costumes, hiring 64
Creative Team 19-28, 69-75,
    79-80, 84-5, 158
Crew 40
Cue list 159
Cues 35, 177, 124, 159
Curtain call 171
Deading 147-154
Design, initial 75
Designer 8, 21-5, 75-6, 111,
    150, 156
Director 8-9, 18, 20, 111-13,
    124, 156, 164, 169-70
Dress Rehearsal 168-70
Dress Rehearsal, safety 100-1
DSM (Deputy Stage Manager)
    34-6, 112, 114, 116-24,
    164-5
Electricity, safety 104-5
Electrics Department 56-9
Equipment, Lighting 56-7
Equipment, Prop making 55
Equipment, Sound 59-61
Equipment, Wardrobe 63
Equipment, Workshop 45-8
Fight 27, 168
Fight Director 27
Final run through 122-4
Finance 125-31
Fire 107
First night 6-7, 170
Fit up 139-140, 145-7
Fit up, Health and Safety 98
Fittings 64, 120

Floor, paint of 145
Flying 40, 140
Focusing 154-6
Freelance 20
Furniture 34, 55, 78
Get-Out 172
Get-Out meeting 101
Get-Out, Safety 101
Gobo 155
Groundplan 136-7
Guidelines (designers) 73
Half hour call 161
Hanging plot 138
Hanging plot, manual
    handling 139
Hard hats 107
Hazardous substances 108-9
Heads of Department (HODs)
    30
Health and Safety 87-9
Health and Safety Policy 89
Health and Safety, Dress
    Rehearsal 100-1
Health and Safety, Electricity
    104-5
Health and Safety, Fit up 98
Health and Safety, Get-Out 101
Health and Safety, Heights
    105-6
Health and Safety, in the
    Workshop 47
Health and Safety, Legislation
    93, 184-6
Health and Safety, Performances
    100
Health and Safety, Rehearsals 97
Health and Safety, Risk

Assessment 79, 90-5, 104
Health and Safety, Technical Rehearsal 98-100
Heights, safety 105-6
Hiring costumes 64
Income 67
Job Description 30, 32, 40-1
Jobs list 147-8
Licensing 95, 97, 107
Lifting regulations 106
Lighting 156-160
Lighting Design 75
Lighting Designer 22-4, 59, 75, 154-60
List, jobs 147-8
List, setting 122-3
LX requirements 78
Manual handling 109
Manual handling, hanging plot 139
Mark up 112
Meet and Greet 110
Meeting, get out 101
Meeting, production 79-80, 84-7
Meeting, progress 135-6
Meeting, white card 76-9
Mission Statement 19
Model 51, 77
Model, white card 76-7
Musical Director 25-6
Noise 108
Notes session 169-70
Opera, Schedule 17, 166
Opera, Sound 62
Opera, Technical Rehearsal 167
Overtime 70, 120, 129
Paintframe 52-3
Painting 50-3
Painting, floor 145
Performances 170-1
Performances, safety 100

Photographs 170
Plot, running 121
Plotting the preset 158
Plotting, lighting 156-60
Plotting, sound 160
Practicals 58
Presenting theatres 10
Preset 158
Problem Solving 141-2
Producing Companies 11
Producing theatres 10-11
Production desk 156, 160
Production meeting 79-80, 84-7
Production Office 28
Production schedule 133-5, 144
Production week 8, 143
Production week, preparing for 136-9
Progress meetings 135-6
Prompt Desk 35, 156, 160
Prompt Script see Book
Prop-making 53-6
Props 34, 55, 78
Props list 119
Rakes stages 94
Read through 111
Recruitment 30-3
References 31
Regulations, lifting 106
Rehearsal calls 117-18
Rehearsal props 120
Rehearsal reports or notes 114-16
Rehearsal room 37-8
Rehearsal, Dress 168-170
Rehearsal, scene change 160
Rehearsals 110-12, 117
Rehearsals, Health and Safety 97
Repertoire 13-14
Repertory theatre 12
Rigging LX 143-5
Risk assessment 79, 90-5, 104

Running plot 121
Safety see Health and Safety
Scale 78
Scene change rehearsal 161
Scene Painting 50-3
Scenic artists 50-3
Scenic construction 44-9
Schedule, build and paint 131-3
Schedule, Opera 17, 166
Schedule, production 133, 144
Schedule, Repertoire 14
Schedule, Repertory 12
Scheduling 131
Script 71
Senior management team 19
Setting list 122-3
Show report 171-2
Sound 59-62, 78, 160
Sound Designer 24-5
Sound Plotting 160
Stage Management 33-40
Stage Manager 33-4, 39, 78, 95, 161, 164, 171
Stage Technicians 40-3
Stagione 13
Superstitions 171
Technical Rehearsal 8, 140-1, 161-7
Technical Rehearsal, Opera 167
Technical Rehearsal, Safety 98-100
The book 35, 116-117, 159, 165
Theatre, repertoire 13
Theatre, repertory 12
Theatres, presenting 10
Theatres, producing 10-11
Touring 172
Wardrobe 62-6, 78
Wardrobe Supervisor 64, 65
White card model meeting 76-9
Working hours 109
Workshop staff 49